MW01231942

Divorce

& Separation

Recovery

10 Stages of Grieving Relationship Loss and Finding Your *Self*

*This book will help you
let go of anger and blame
and get on with living
your life more fully*

By Dwight Webb, Ph.D.

PETER E. RANDALL PUBLISHER
Portsmouth, New Hampshire • 1996

Peter E. Randall Publisher
P.O. Box 4726
Portsmouth, NH 03802

ISBN 0-914339-55-9

This book is dedicated to Cherry Parker,
who taught me that emotions are too precious to waste
on blame and anger.

Contents ❧

Acknowledgements ✍

Thanks to…

Cherry Parker for prizing the optimism in me.

John Krumboltz, Arnold Lazarus, and William Glasser for lessons on pragmatism.

David Van Nuys and Bert Whetstone who gave me continuing encouragement to stay with the book.

Karen Hailson, Susan Stewart, and Judy Randall for early readings and editing suggestions.

Kay Munson, who deciphered my handwriting and put out a readable manuscript, only to be presented with re-writes and re-writes of re-writes. Wisely, she encouraged me to get ouside help.

Foreword

Who among us has not known the heartbreak of a faded relationship? Who has not had to bear, at one time or another, the advice of well-meaning friends to just buck up and move on, that there are other fish in the sea, that this loss is just clearing the way for an even better relationship? Easier said than done when you are feeling as though you have just lost that one special person who somehow gives your life meaning.

The book you hold in your hands represents a miracle of personal transformation. My friend, Dwight Webb, is one of those rare individuals who knows how to turn lemons into lemonade. The lemonade-making process is not always as easy as it might sound, however, because first the lemons get squeezed. Hard. I remember the anguish that Dwight went through during the breakup described in the beginning of the book. His heart and his soul were being squeezed by a circumstance beyond his control. It was the death of a relationship upon which he had pinned his hopes and his dreams. It was the death of a piece of himself.

This book underscores the archetypal cycle of death and rebirth. Dwight went down into the pit, endured the agonies of loss, cried his tears, fought his demons, and emerged, I am happy to report, a reborn and wiser hero.

According to Joseph Campbell, the successful hero emerges from the journey with a boon, or gift, which can be shared with others. In this case, that boon is this book, which was born out of pain and confusion, that raw and primal stuff. I was in contact with Dwight during the time that he was writing the book and had the opportunity to read the original manuscript. The changes that it has undergone since that first effort are quite extraordinary. I have been impressed by the way he sought out critical feedback on the manuscript and its underlying ideas, and the tenacity with which, over a period of years, he kept reworking and refining it until it became the fine product we see today. I know that he wrestled mightily, not only with his own story and how to make meaning out of it, but also with existing theory and the process of letting his own theoretical insights emerge. The word, wrestle, perhaps communicates too much of a sense of strain, because as his own healing progressed, there was also, I think, an element of play in it.

It will be apparent on the dust cover that Dwight is a professor and a counselor. However, this book is intended for a lay audience, rather than an academic one. Nevertheless, it is solidly grounded in psychological theory. In particular, his opening chapter on "Stages of Grieving" draws heavily on the work of Kubler-Ross, who has written extensively about the stages of grief in response to the death of a loved-one. Dwight goes beyond her work to further elaborate the model and to extend it into the area of relationship loss. The model advanced by Kubler-Ross lists five stages. Building upon that framework, Dwight nicely distinguishes between loss by death and relationship loss and goes on to delineate ten stages of grieving and healing. Subsequent chapters build on the foundation of this model and deftly interweave into the fabric of the book insights from Rogerian, Humanistic, Transpersonal, Reality Therapy, and Learning Theory perspectives.

It would be a mistake, I think, to dismiss this work as "merely" another self-help book. Just as teaching is a high-calling, so is the broad dissemination of psychological insight and knowledge, when founded on solid fact and sound theory.

I hope this book finds the wide audience it truly deserves. As a therapist and educator, myself, it will definitely be a tool that I will use in working with clients and students who are grieving the loss of a relationship. I know of no other resource that deals with these issues in a way that is so sound and yet so personal, compassionate, and engaging. I think that readers who are, themselves, moving through the loss of an important relationship will find inspiration and concrete guidance here.

This book is true to the trajectory of my friend, Dwight's, field work—the exploration, explication, and teaching of themes having to do with authenticity, love, and courage. This life's mission is seen in his closing invitation to the reader:

I invite you to join me in the challenge...to claim your own strength and the courage to discover your own best way of expressing your love.

—*David Van Nuys, Ph.D.*
Sonoma State University
October 1995

Introduction ꣸

Man does not simply exist,
but always decides what his existence will be,
what he will become in the next moment.
...every human being has the freedom to
choose at any instant.
—Victor Frankl[1]

The greatest freedom we have is to choose. It was Victor
Frankl who reminded us so powerfully of this truth when he
wrote about our ultimate freedom "...to choose one's attitude
in any given set of circumstances, to choose one's own way."
Although we know we are free in this way, we don't always
act to exercise our freedom. This book will encourage you to
claim this very basic freedom. Choosing requires taking
responsibility for the outcomes in your life. Often, people find
it easier to choose not to choose, and avoid taking responsibility. When we do this, we blame or scapegoat others, and
identify ourselves as victims, occasionally comforted by people's sympathy. Beware of such a trap! This book will encourage you to take responsibility for your life choices and to take
those risks knowing that some choices will be difficult, some
painful, and not all outcomes of your choices will yield per-
fection. Choosing is a life attitude which is expressed in the
willingness to travel the path of personal responsibility.

Choose Love Because It is In Your Best Interest

As you meet your challenges of being single, you will be faced
with many choices. My first challenge for you to consider is to
invite you to choose love.

Choose love, it is the path upon which you will find peace

Choose love, it is therein that you will find strength
Choose love, it is upon that foundation that you
will build new dreams
                                    ...and make them come true.

Why should you be loving when you feel angry? This is an important question. The answer is straight forward. Be loving because it is in *your* best interest. It is *your* well-being which is the most important focus of your healing and development as a person. This book will try to convince you that love is healthier for you than hate or bitterness. Blaming others will simply get in your way and be a burden you don't need or want.

You are probably asking yourself:

- Why should I love the person who betrayed my deepest trust?
- What am I supposed to do with my hurt?
                                       my anger?
                                       my loss?
- What am I supposed to do with my broken heart?
                                       my broken promises?
                                       my broken dreams?

These are important questions, and there are more:
- How will I survive?
- Can I make it on my own?
- Will I ever love again?
- Will I dare to trust again?

All these questions and many more will be answered in time as you move through your grieving of the loss of your relationship.

I want you to know at the outset that your answers will be most certainly and most enormously affected by your attitude, your beliefs, your choices and your behaviors. This book will help you set your course of recovery on paths which will create healing of your deepest wounds from your loss, and open your heart to your best options and opportunities for wellness, vitality and the happiness which you deserve.

It is okay to be angry. Your anger in fact stems from self love. You are in effect saying: "...I have been wronged and I won't be treated this way." Your anger is protecting you from further hurt, a kind of damage control mechanism to defend you against deeper devastation. Legitimate anger is quite appropriate when there has been betrayal and thoughtless insensitive circumstances which have been dealt to you against your wishes and against your faith and commitment to the relationship.

Anger will not serve you however, if it becomes your weapon for revenge. If your motive is trying to get back and even the score, your anger, like a volcano, will destroy everything in its path and leave you quite barren & smoldering. This book will help you examine all of your feelings, including anger, and will help you to express yourself in healthy and productive ways. It will help you to avoid blame and bitterness and the accompanying toxicity which prevents you from getting on with your life.

Being the One Who is Left

If you were the one who was left, you no doubt sensed some time ago that your relationship was in trouble, and perhaps dismissed these thoughts because they were so upsetting. There is usually one partner who wants out more than the other, and there is always more pain for the one who doesn't want the separation or divorce. The tendency of course is to blame the leaving person, and while this may be fair, it will not help you in the long run to allow yourself to be so victimized. Better to admit that you had some part in it. How did all this chaos happen? It will be helpful for you to review your struggles which preceded your break-up in order to gain as much perspective as you can. Here is a beginning checklist you can ask yourself, but don't stop with this list. You should ask yourself many more questions to explore your unique situation thoroughly.

> What caused the stress?
>> job?
>> money worries?
>> another lover?
>> jealousy?
>> possessiveness?
>> alcohol?
>> lack of sensitivity?
>> not listening, not validating , not understanding each other?
> All or several of the above?
> How did your children or lack of children figure in?
> How did your in-laws or other family members figure in?
> What about other outside intrusions?

Once you begin to see a more complete picture of your situation, take a look at how the two of you did with communicating with each other in facing these issues. Finally the most important question will emerge: *What will you do differently next time?*

If There are Children

There are huge issues to be dealt with in any break-up, and everything is compounded when there are children involved. Questions of loyalties, child support and simply day-to-day coping emotionally and financially can be overwhelming. As parents, the most important agreement to work out with your former partner is the overarching question: "What is in the best interest of our children?" If you both can commit to this as a non-negotiable principle which will guide your decisions and actions, you will always place the developmental needs of your children first. This is particularly important for the non-residential parent. Each parent must pay careful attention to his and her part in creating clear and effective communication as you figure out the best way to work together for the benefit of the children. Barbara Peeks[2], a family therapist & school counselor, has developed a parents' script as an intervention in working with divorced families. She meets individually with the parents and asks them to set aside their animosity about husband and wife issues for the sake of the children. In this meeting they are asked to reach agreement about the following 15 statements as a basis for discussion with each other in support of their children.

The parents' script:

1. We both love you very much and we will continue to love you.
2. You were conceived with love, which is something that can never change.
3. Our divorce is not your fault and you did nothing to cause it.
4. We will always help and protect you.
5. We cannot get back together as husband and wife. Do not hope for it.
6. We are divorcing as husband and wife, not as mother and father.
7. We will communicate and work together on matters concerning you.
8. We will not say bad things about each other.
9. You will not have to choose between us.
10. We will support each other's rules.
11. We want you to do well in school and life.
12. We do not expect you to have problems because we are divorcing and we do not expect you to use our divorce as an excuse for problems in your life.
13. We do not know all the details about the future, but we will tell you as soon as we know.
14. You will be able to visit all your grandparents, aunts and uncles and they will not say bad things about either of us.

15. You have our permission to mind, respect, and love your other parent, step-parent or significant others.

Be aware that in all matters dealing with your former mate, your own attitude will have the most fundamental effect on your relationship. It will effect everything about the motives and outcomes of your communication. Don't shoot yourself in the foot or otherwise sabotage yourself because your angry feelings are getting in the way. Letting anger dominate your life is like letting the tail wag the dog.

This book will not address the myriad dimensions of necessary coping with issues which involve children. Rather I will focus on *your* healing in grieving the loss of your relationship and what you need to do to get on with your life.

Challenge Yourself

It is painful to remember the dream you shared in your courtship days as you were falling in love and getting ready for marriage. This is however, a pain that I recommend you face, because it will be healthy for you to revisit that memory in order to re-kindle the spirit of your more open, sensual, sexual, romantic and playful self. In those courtship days, you were full of hope and possibility. You need to know that you are still capable of that heart-opening connection because it will help you to re-connect your loving vitality which has been dampened down with hurt, anger, bitterness and probably some cynicism and self-doubt. At some level, we always know that life will not be one big bowl of cherries; that there will be stress and differences to work on, and we trust that this will unfold as it should without inordinate disruption. Trust yourself to get through these stressors and to live joyfully again. When love is new, we tell ourselves that we can make our dream of "living happily ever after" come true. It is important to awaken and renew this trust in yourself and your own sense of possibilities; it will make your life more abundant. We all need our dreams, our hopes and expectancies to set us on our best course. We need to nurture ourselves with such faith.

I love that very old Irish blessing which says in part:

...May the road rise up to meet you...

And I want to say in response:

May you also rise up to meet the road. There will be many paths which will present themselves to you.

Preface:
A Piece of My Story

This book is about me, and it's about you;
those of us who have been left when
we didn't want it or expect it.

I called her Winter. She was (as I thought at the time), the love of my life. She was more than my lover, she was my all-kinds-of-weather-best-friend-ever. I felt more love in this relationship than any I had ever known. At times I felt adored. For the better part of six years we danced on the planet with passion and with joy.

Winter and I were never legally married although we both felt that the mated bond we shared was greater than any legal document could attest to. I assumed that we would be married when the paperwork of my divorce was completed and we figured out how we could integrate our marriage in a way that would allow me to be as good a parent as I could be to my four sons. Difficult circumstances.

Daring to Dream

Most of us want to share our lives intimately with a partner. There is a strong urge to mate that is built into our wiring for survival. This desire to bond is first experienced as images which we create while we daydream about our future.

In our daydreaming we picture a family, children, friends, adventures, houses becoming homes, and all the details which surround these images. In our lives we move unconsciously toward that which we can imagine.

I had dared to dream again and felt mated, coupled, in love, and adored. I was full of pictures of blissful togetherness in our future. I was in the spell of the powerful myth which says that we will find our true love and live happily ever after. For men it is that image of one "princess" or the "goddess" who has taken us as their prince, their hero. This is a mythical love for both partners. For women we hear stories about "prince charming" and "knights on white horses." It is the "Cinderella Complex." These myths are part of our collective unconsciousness. The universality of these myths is probably both a) learned from our folk tales including movies, television, songs, and books, and b) genetic in the sense that we strive to bond with the most beautiful (sexually attractive) mate we can find in order to ensure the desirability of our offspring and thus, our survival.

I suspect that most people hold onto these myths or dreams most of their lives. Some may even manage to make them come true for most of a lifetime. It is important not to reject these myths. To say that such blissful states cannot be is to take a very jaded view of our possibilities.

In retrospect, I can see how being jaded might have protected me from my hurt by limiting my involvement, my expectations, and my hopes and dreams. Still in all, I don't think it is a good idea to put blinders on our sense of possibilities.

For lots of reasons which will be written about throughout this book, my relationship with Winter, my dreams, and the "prince and princess myth" all began to fade at the end of our sixth year. After three months of struggle, Winter decided she needed to leave and find a place of her own.

Even though I could see it coming, I was stunned.

Sadness came over me like a fog that wouldn't burn off. I felt hurt, frustration, anger, and a sense of helplessness. Why would she leave all the joy we had shared? I was flooded with confusion, crying inside, raising self-doubting questions.

What went wrong?
Where do I go from here?

I felt betrayed and rejected. Too much sadness to let in the anger. Too much confusion. Too deep to let all my feelings into awareness at once. It was like a death had occurred. I had no idea how sad I would feel. It shook the very core of me.

The Male Conspiracy Against Feeling

Men get strong messages which say:

Don't be vulnerable.
Don't share your feelings with others...better yet,
    don't even let your feelings into consciousness.

Most men have become card-carrying members of the conspiracy against expressing feelings. To conspire literally means "to breathe together." For men this means also holding your breath and holding onto your feelings. The survival lesson men and women learn from an early age is that when we are burned we avoid hot stoves. There are strong cultural forces with messages like:

Be careful.
Are you sure you can trust again?

We learn to rationalize and deny our feelings (the stiff-upper-lip syndrome), and our self-talk says:

Life goes on.
You'd better just get it together.

So how in the hell is a man supposed to grieve? To grieve is to feel, and men are not supposed to feel, they are supposed to cope. The fact is, I had been badly hurt and I was flooded with feelings.

How do I break out of this dilemma? I have just lost the

love of my life, and I am feeling devastated. I am incredibly sad, and very confused, and this backboned-stiff-upper-lip macho voice says:

> *Be strong.*
> *Keep your cool.*
> *Don't show your hurt.*
> *Carry on as if nothing much has happened.*

My heart said something else.

I didn't want to cry, but I did. I didn't want to get angry, but I was. When I was alone, I could let down a little and feel sad. But somehow when I was with others I needed to put on a mask which told the world that I was doing fine. So, I was torn between hiding from my feelings and wanting to shout: "God Damn it! What happened?"

Learning to Be Cool

Often, what we learn in our growing-up experience is not at all useful or helpful in getting us through our emotional pain. For example:

- We may learn to withdraw in order to protect ourselves from hurt.
- We may learn to strike back and punish.
- We all too often learn to blame others for what happens to us, and in so doing we fail to learn to take responsibility for ourselves.
- We mostly learn to bury or disown our feelings.

While the above examples are especially true for men in our culture, these are very human behaviors which are highly reinforced for both men and women. The good news is that we are on the verge of a consciousness shift where we are coming to see that these responses are no longer serving us well in our relationships at home, at work, or at play. We can be much more direct, more honest, more expressive.

Unlearning

The real challenge for all of us is: How do we unlearn "being cool"? How do we let go of worn out beliefs and attitudes? More importantly:

> *How do I let myself feel?*
> *How do I let myself grieve?*
> *How do I recover from my loss, and cope with*
>   *change and create the life I want for myself?*

Trying to answer these questions led me to write this book. Throughout this book I give my perspective of how I experienced my own grieving. While these are my thoughts and ideas, I hope they will make sense to you and shed some light upon the path you are traveling.

I believe that knowing is better than not knowing. If I can show you as readers, a process that you are in and moving through, I believe it will help you through your grieving passage and shape the outcomes of your recovery. Knowing and understanding more about your feelings and your movement through your own grieving process will be helpful to you. Such self-understanding is a beginning in discovering your options and making decisions which are in your best interest.

This book tells my story about my loss and how I got through it in time. It will invite you to:

- see that grieving your relationship loss is a normal and necessary process for your recovery and continuing growth.
- discover your own personal way of grieving your loss, and learn about the beginning, middle, and completion phases in the process of your recovery.
- claim the reality and legitimacy of all that you are feeling.
- postpone judgment about your feelings until you can look at them, begin to understand them, and express them in a healing way.

- see how some of your own natural defenses such as denial, anger, and blame get overplayed in grieving and slowdown or stop your grieving process.
- examine your own progress in your grieving by providing a road map of the territory.
- participate actively in your own recovery process by providing exercises to personalize your involvement and commitment to your own well-being.

I assume that you are reading this book because you are open to and invested in your own growth, even at the risk of feeling your pain. At some level, you know that the greater risk is in not letting yourself experience your feelings. I also assume that you don't want to sabotage your own best interests, and that you are willing to cooperate with your survival instincts which will guide you to do the work you need to do to get through to full recovery.

In the following chapter, I present the ten stages of grieving that I discovered on my recovery journey. The rest of the book is organized around moving through these ten stages. As you go through the book and find yourself at various stages, you may see where you have become bogged down in anger, denial or blame, or are just spinning your wheels in pointless bargaining. You will see how these ten stages serve you, and how there may be pitfalls and places where you get stuck along the way. Your growth and recovery will favor your being unstuck.

You have the capacity to chart your course and shape your experience as you move through your grieving. I am hopeful that this book will help you make choices which move you along healthy pathways in your recovery from loss.

I. Stages of Grieving ∽

To lose your mate when all your hopes and dreams
are focused on sharing your life with this person
is one of the most painful experiences anyone can know.
It is in some ways the ultimate loss.

Being in love for me is being in a strong emotional and spiritually bonded relationship. When Winter broke that bond, I felt as if every facet where our blended energies connected had been ripped open. I experienced a stark aloneness in painful contrast to the joy we had shared. I felt a gray, flat, quiet void where there had been rich colors and textures. I felt silence and emptiness where there had been music and fullness in our intimacy. I was enormously confused, and profoundly sad.

I wondered:

> *Will there ever again in my life be such love...such*
> *a soul mate...best friend?*

The Pain of Aloneness

In the early days of finding myself alone, my world felt like it had been turned upside down. My trust, my love, my hope for a shared dream had been shattered.

I asked myself:

> *What could I have done differently?*
> *Maybe there is something wrong with me?*

I needed to keep asking these and other similar questions even though my answers were not always clear or complete.

This void in my life was extremely unsettling for me. I didn't like sleeping alone. I didn't like coming home to a house that was empty and would remain empty. Loneliness was an unwelcome intruder. Eating my evening meal alone did not hold a candle to the joy Winter and I had shared at such times with warmth, with laughter, with touching. With Winter, I felt spiritually nourished. She had been my best friend and my partner through sunrises and sunsets. We played tennis, skied the snow, sailed the waters, and celebrated the richness of life with good friends. Facing my solitude, I experienced a huge loss of the intimacy which so nurtured me.

I was in shock, and the only way I could really deal with this pain was to just refuse to believe that this relationship was really over. I put on my denial mask in facing my world because I had to believe that Winter and I would make it in time. I was stunned. I had no road map for where I was going or how I would get through this uncharted territory of being alone. Life would be different for me now. It wasn't just being alone, it was being apart—separate from my joyous intimate partner. It was the furthest thing from what I wanted.

Only in hindsight could I begin to see what I was going through. Not until I had come through my shock and denial did I come to discover that there was a process with different stages and parts to my grieving. While everything was not lock step, crisp, or clear, I did sort out my experience in ways which may be summarized in the following chart, "Ten Stages of Grieving Relationship Loss."

Rejection

Losing a relationship by rejection is a more personal affront than losing a relationship by death. Rejection is an assault on your self-esteem. The range and character of your feelings and experiences may be similar in many respects to loss due to death, but there are important differences. Even though I've

TEN STAGES OF
GRIEVING RELATIONSHIP LOSS

Early Stages:
1. Shock and disbelief
2. Denial   • Flooded with feelings
3. Anger and hidden feelings
4. Negotiating for change   • Trying to hold on

Middle Stages:
5. Low point and turning point • Facing the truth
6. Understanding

Later Stages:
7. Acceptance   • Keys to letting go
8. Forgiveness
9. Making a plan   • Creating positive
                                      experience

Recovery:
10. Taking action   • Asserting personal
                                      growth

Credit is given to Elizabeth Kubler-Ross[3] for the ideas which form the framework for the grieving process. She lists five stages of grieving: (1) shock and disbelief, (2) denial, (3) anger, (4) bargaining, and (5) acceptance. Relationship loss—while similar to a loss by death—has distinct differences. Just the fact that your ex-mate is alive changes the nature of your hopes and expectations.

been rejected, as long as the other person is alive, I may hold on to hope, and have some thoughts and expectations that things will work out. We all know of cases where couples have gotten back together.

When your ex-partner is still alive, it makes it easier to deny that it is all over. We hold on to hope even though it may be false hope. Even though it seems headed that way, we deny that it is going to end up with separation. It is normal to deny and hold on to hope. It serves to stave off the pain. The trick is to not get stuck in denial. In time, you will face whatever the truth is, and get on with completing the cycle of grieving.

Anger is also quite different when there is loss by rejection. There is a greater danger and tendency toward blaming and bitterness when your ex-mate is alive and continuing to choose to be separate from you.

Grieving As a Process

When you are reminded of your lost love, do you:

> *Get angry?*
> *Get sad?*
> *Feel like a loser?*
> *Feel embarrassed?*
> *All of the above?*

Do you wonder:

> *Will I ever find love again?*
> *Can I make it on my own?*

Grieving is a process, a normal and necessary process for recovery from loss. There is a beginning, a middle time, and an ending to your grief. This process goes on to greater or lesser degrees for weeks, months, and sometimes years.

Be assured that it does not take forever. But also know that it is important to keep the process moving. Sometimes we paralyze ourselves in grieving for too long a time. Either we talk ourselves into thinking that we can never get over our hurt and our anger which we feel from being abandoned, or we delude ourselves with dreams from the past, hoping beyond hope that some miracle will turn things around. These pauses in the process are normal for all of us as we sort out the pain of our sadness. The trick is to not remain paralyzed in such ways which prolong our passage, and cause us to not function effectively.

It is very human to grieve when you have experienced a loss in your life. Such grieving is universal, and transcends the boundaries of age, culture, and gender. While the ideas in this book are from a male point of view, I believe that the process of grieving outlined here will apply to people of all ages, and to women as well as men.

The movement through these stages is a little like being in a swimming pool and moving into deeper water as you feel safe. There is trial and error going on all the time. There are no well-defined boundaries, although the ten stages do have a loose kind of sequencing which may help you in understanding this very natural human process toward healing. Each stage highlights a major theme of the process through grieving toward recovery. Grieving by definition is simply the title word given to all the feelings which we experience as a result of our personal loss. Becoming vulnerable to your grief is simply saying to yourself: "I have been hurt. I have feelings. It's important to express my feelings."

Stages Cycle Upward

Grieving stages are cyclical. There is a falling to a low point when you bottom out. And there is a climbing out. The nice thing about hitting the bottom is that things can only go up from this point. The climb is a turning toward rebuilding your life. When we are in the middle of our own grieving, it is not always clear what we should do next. We may not see how we can understand, or accept, much less forgive. When I was in shock and disbelief, I would not look at my anger, and when I got into my anger, I wasn't interested in understanding or accepting. I needed to feel my feelings. Only later was I ready to understand, accept, and forgive.

In the final stages, your willingness to choose and to act become more important as you take responsibility for making your life what you want it to be. Throughout this book, I encourage you to focus on your choices and make commitments to those actions necessary to get you through to recovery.

There is no precise timetable for moving through these stages of grieving, and you will have to depend on your own inner sensing to know if your movement is right for you. From time to time you will feel yourself bogging down in a particular stage. This is your inner wisdom trying to wake you up to look ahead to the next stages.

Getting to Forgiveness

It is important that you understand that forgiveness comes only after the earlier issues—particularly anger and blame—have been faced and dealt with. All the earlier stages must be experienced before you will be ready to forgive.

In most cases of relationship loss there has been no evil intent. I don't believe that even the betrayal of vows is evil, although I would not argue that betrayal is morally right, and I would never advocate it as the high road for human experience. Betrayal happens. People are not perfectly evolved yet, and people make mistakes and bad choices. These things I can forgive. These mistakes are imperfections and blemishes on our full understanding of ourselves as we evolve toward awareness.

Forgiveness is an important choice you can make in the later stages of your grieving, it will be your final letting go of blame. It will mean you no longer need to hold someone else responsible for your circumstances or feelings.

I believe there can be no complete healing or full recovery until you can let go of all the bitterness you are feeling for the person you once loved. I want you to know that to forgive or not to forgive is a choice you have. I am encouraging you to make the choice to forgive and to be free of holding on to blame. Forgive because it is going to make *you* feel better.

Stronger than Before

There are healthy ways of going through your grieving, and there are human frailties which may block you or keep you stuck for a time. This book will show you healthy ways to complete your stages of grieving. It will point out ways and places where you may get stuck. You will come to see that your grieving is a cycle, because you do bottom out, and you do come up again. The goal is to come up stronger, smarter, and happier. We know that when we get physically hurt there will be bruises and fractures, but that our bodies will heal in time. Recovery from a devastating psychological injury is also a process that takes time.

Recovery is ongoing. From the moment that you are knocked down, you will be responding with efforts to recover from the impact and the trauma. Each moment and each new day there is a movement toward trying to achieve balance. We ask ourselves:

> *What can I learn from this?*
> *How can I become stronger?*

It is not just recovery to where you were, but beyond to a stronger and clearer state of consciousness with greater stability and balance.

Choosing Health

If you can see the healing path, you can choose it. Seeing yourself in this ten-stage process of grieving is an important first step in taking a more active part in moving through the stages. You will be challenged to examine your attitudes and behaviors and discard those which are not working for you. Finding yourself on your healing path and seeing the landmarks which will lead you out of your confusion and pain is a great advantage you can take.

Yesterday, I was canoeing with my son David on the Penobscot River, and, in addition to it being a beautiful day, we had the advantage of having both the current and the wind at our backs. I hope this book will be a current for you on your journey through these ten stages and provide a warm, gentle, and encouraging breeze for you. Like most journeys, yours will require you to leave the shore, to set a course, and to paddle.

I am hopeful that you will move through your
grieving with all possible speed and in good health.

II. Going Inside ᔓ

Making Alone Time

The first thing you need to do is to create some time for yourself. Find a quiet place to be calm and to just be with yourself. A time to read this book and to reflect and be with your feelings. Let this be a time you choose as a way of being good to yourself. Set aside time to focus on getting through your grieving.

Above all else, this will be a time to face and acknowledge all your feelings. It is often difficult for us to be with our feelings, or to know them and express them. One way we avoid our feelings is to keep ourselves constantly busy with other things. We have learned to hold back and to control our feelings because letting ourselves experience our deeper feelings can be frightening and unsettling. We hide our feelings because to express them is to run the risk of being further rejected or embarrassed in the presence of others who may be uncomfortable with us when we express our sadness, anger, or confusion. We too often parade behind this self-designed mask, and block ourselves from experiencing and understanding our legitimate feelings as if they weren't there, or didn't count for much. There is discomfort in facing our pain, and this is still another reason we avoid letting ourselves feel. We can manufacture lots of reasons not to feel. Setting time aside to just let yourself be, and to discover your own feelings is facing this discomfort and setting aside the mask.

Feeling Deeply

Tears are difficult to express in our culture. This is particularly true for men,[4] but it's also true for many women. We learn to fight back our tears and keep our heads held high... "chin up." Being alone with your feelings is to open yourself to your sadness, and your tears are a very legitimate expression of these feelings. Releasing your feelings makes it easier for you to return to other responsibilities. It's holding on to your feelings that keeps you burdened. Your alone time is a safe place to begin to give yourself permission to feel, and you will discover that it is a sign of your love of life that you can feel deeply and care so much. Celebrate it! Look to the other side of pain and remember that you also are capable of experiencing great joy.

Keeping a Journal

An important activity in your alone time is to "think out loud to yourself" by writing in your journal. Journal writing in these private, safe times is a way to sort through the chaos of your feelings.

I found that if I didn't take time for myself, I was just holding up my brave mask and focusing all of my time and energy in my outer world of daily activities. I discovered when I took time with myself and sat down to write, that I began to get messages from my feelings. As I opened up and began to listen to that self under the mask, I found that I could accept my wide range of feelings and still return to the control I needed for functioning, and in a fresh and less burdened way.

Keeping a journal is a creative way for exploring your inner world. It really isn't any more complicated than setting aside time to do it, just as you do for eating, brushing your teeth, or a myriad of other activities and rituals. Your writing or reflections don't have to be in a fancy notebook. Use whatever is handy and easy for you. You may even want to jot notes to yourself on a grocery bag or on your calendar. Whatever works for you.

Some of the material which came forth as I wrote in my journal had such power that I was a bit uneasy with my own intensity at first. For example, when I felt depressed and angry a voice in my head would say:

> *I'm a jerk for letting myself get so involved! I'm*
> *really pissed at Winter for taking me for granted,*
> *and for giving up on us after all we've shared.*

What seemed to help me in times like these was to go out into my woods and knock off dead limbs from pine trees. Splitting wood also helped me to release my pent-up anguish.

At other times another voice would counter that and say:

> *She is only doing what she needs to do.*
> *Let her go with your blessing.*

It was important for me to give expression to all these inner thoughts because it made me feel better. Giving voice to my feelings and writing them in my journal, helped me sort through my confusion.

I suggest that when you write in your journal you just let whatever wants to bubble up come out. Follow whatever emerges in your stream of consciousness, and you will begin to see where you may be stuck, and what you need to do.

Let your journal be a time to record a dream, for dreams are a rich voice of your inner world. Let it be a time to draw pictures, write poetry, and to remember. Use your journal to paste in quotations from writings that speak to you, or cut out pictures, cartoons, symbols, images, and the like. Anything that has meaning for you will resonate and open up channels for your healing energy.

Your journal is a record, like a yardstick; it shows you where you've been. From time to time you may read over earlier entries and see how you have moved on or to see just how you are stuck with certain recurring issues. This kind of self-reflection over time allows you to see your own grieving process, your thoughts and your behavior. It is a beginning of your being both the observer and the person observed. It is a new way of understanding yourself.

Find a Good, Caring Listener

While alone time is important, it is also important to sort out your confusions and sadness in the presence of someone who cares for you, is accepting, and trys to understand. What you don't need at this time is to be cut off from your feelings by too much reassurance, advise, story telling of their experience, or lots of questions. What you do need is to be listened to and honored for who you are, to be accepted in all your pain and anguish, in all your confusion.

This listening, caring, and accepting person can be a friend, a family member, or it can be a counselor. And, it can be all of the above. The main ingredient in this relationship is trust. Find someone with whom you feel safe to disclose and share your feelings.

Risking Being Open

There really are lots of people you can trust! Many people believe the opposite: that it is not safe to be open and to share your feelings with others. No doubt they have come to that belief because of the family or friendship patterns of their earlier lives. If this is your belief, I'm asking you to challenge it, and telling you that it is working against you not for you.

The more open we are, the less burden of secrecy we carry, the more trust we extend, the less guarded, defensive and self-protective we have to be. There will be less cover-up and pretense, less denial, less rationalization, less need for smokescreens to hide our honest feelings if we dare to be open. Being honest and forthright has the effect of building stronger and more meaningful relationships. The more truth, the more health.

While there is much that you can do in dealing with your personal grief in quiet and private ways, sharing at appropriate times with friends and family draws their caring into your strength. You build a support network of well-wishers, encouragers, and people who respect you for your openness, honesty, and courage, for facing—not diminishing—a very important issue in your life, namely your significant loss.

Getting Through Your Own Resistance

You very likely will resist journal writing and other commitments to be good to yourself. The way through this resistance is to first acknowledge it, and look at what it is doing for you. Is it serving you? Is it keeping you protected from experiencing the pain of your feelings? You may even resist looking at your resistance. You may hear strong rationalizing voices which say:

> *Who has time for it?*
> *I have no time for myself!*
> *I'm too busy with my schedule and the kids!*

Other voices of resistance might sound like:

> *I don't want to look at all this stuff, I just want it*
> *to all go away, and all to be over!*
> (magical thinking)

The point is, you need to grieve. It's an important part of being human and healing. You have had a loss, and you need to acknowledge it to get over it. You can move through your feelings with more clarity and completion if you are willing to look at them and experience them. Feelings don't go away if they are buried.

Since you are a unique person with a distinct set of circumstances, you will go through your grieving process in your own way and in your own time frame. I want you to know that you can influence that way, and that time frame, by what you choose to challenge, to explore, and to do for yourself. Listen to yourself with a non-judgmental ear. Set your own goals and priorities. Then make the decisions necessary for reaching these. Your intuitive wisdom wants you to be well and happy.

Be gentle with yourself, and know that to be open to your own experience of feelings and to your choices, is to live more freely, and more fully. In the long run, this openness is the only way out of pain, and your best path to growth. To choose not to be open is to die in some psychological or spiritual sense. It is to put up walls and barriers and to see life in rigid, overly protective terms. Try to get through your own resistance.

Change Is Hard

We often fool ourselves into thinking that the easier road is not to change, because there is comfort and safety in being our old regular predictable selves. It's this old-shoe identity which, hopefully, gets us accepted, acknowledged, respected, even loved for being the person we are. We find our place and way of being with our circle of friends and family. These issues of consistency in our identity are tremendously important in maintaining and building predictable relationships. They are the behaviors and attitudes which define us.

The bad news is that if we don't examine these attitudes and behaviors, we may build boxes for ourselves with very tight boundaries. We may think that these boundaries protect us in terms of standing up for what we believe in. It is more likely that we are standing in fear of the unknown and unfamiliar. Fear and insecurity drive us to put on blinders and close out our options. Fixed patterns, black-and-white thinking, and other forms of rigidity do not favor growth. When I see people with narrow points of view, who are rigid and dogmatic in their thinking—people afraid to take the necessary risks in discovering themselves—I think of them as having a severe case of hardening of the categories. This has been referred to as psychosclerosis, and like hardening of the arteries, it can be lethal in causing a psychological death. There is no growth without openness. Growth means taking the risk to change worn-out patterns of behavior.

The good news is that all you have to do is be willing to look within, make some decisions about how you want things to be for you, and then line up with all the opportunities which present themselves to you. Simple it is, but easy it is not. To change takes effort. It takes concentration, discipline, and the courage to face the unknown, trusting that within the unknown also lies the opportunity.

Opportunities

We are presented every day with opportunities. There is always the opportunity to choose. I'm reminded of an old Eagles song where the lyrics say:

> So oftentimes it happens that we live our lives in
> chains and we never even know we have the key.[5]

You can choose the opportunity to grow, and not be beaten down by life's circumstances. You can choose to love life, and the living of your own life to your fullest potential. Recovery begins with self-love because this is the foundation for the love of life.

Be open to the challenge of seeing your choices as opportunities. Think about all your attitudes and behaviors as having options which are up for periodic review. Ask yourself: "What are my best pathways to recovery? What do I need to do to move on to a happy and full life?"

Exercises

Throughout this book, and at the end of this and other chapters, you will find suggested activities and exercises designed to illuminate your healing path. These are meant to get you involved with, and to find ways to tap into, your own intuitive healing energy. While there are specific instructions for these, you may wish to create your own exercises and discover your best way for focusing and releasing. Visualization, relaxation, affirmations, and journal writing are some of the techniques for altering your attitudes and belief systems. These exercises are simple in many respects, but they are also profound because you are opening yourself up to change, and presenting a challenge to yourself. Any time you attempt to change your belief systems, it is an enormous challenge, and requires you to choose to commit yourself to the task.

Use this book, don't just read it. Take this opportunity to be active in your own growth process.

> *Do the exercises in the book.*
> *Write in the margins*
> *and keep a journal*
> *or a notebook*
> *for your feelings,*
> *opinions,*
> *musings,*
> *reflections,*
> *insights,*
> *values,*
> *and decisions.*
> *They are uniquely yours.*
> *Own them,*
> *and celebrate your willingness*
> *to change.*

Doing the suggested exercises will help you to focus your energies on images of positive change. It has been known for some time that the images we hold in our heads tend to come true. Our unconscious mind finds ways of moving us toward what we deeply want and need, and what we can imagine or visualize for ourselves. Your task is to be open to this process and to make a disciplined effort to set aside time to do the exercises as part of being good to yourself.

Notice that whether or not you take time for yourself, it is a choice you have. If you don't make time for yourself, it is simply that you place less priority on this dimension of your life right now. To some extent in our culture, we all learn not to give ourselves personal attention. You can break these cultural restrictions if you choose to.

SUGGESTED EXERCISES

Visualization & Affirmations:

First, find a quiet, relaxing place and sit comfortably or lie down on your back and make yourself peaceful.*

Take several deep breaths, and picture your tension leaving each time you exhale. Now as you inhale, feel a cleansing vitality coming into you. Feel a relaxing and peaceful energy flowing easily with each breath. Continue to breathe deeply and to relax and feel peaceful and confident.

Say these affirmations to yourself:

- I am in the beginning stages of designing a new life for myself.
- I am beginning to become aware of the old patterns and attitudes which have kept me stuck, and I will let go of these.
- I am beginning today with a willingness to find new ways to grow.
- I can choose and make a commitment to take steps toward being good to myself.
- I will allow myself to feel my feelings.
- I will share my struggles with a trusted, caring, accepting listener.
- I will do the exercises in this book and be open to new ways and to growth.

---

*You may wish to put on soft background music, meditative or trance tapes are available at most music stores. They are enormously helpful in accessing this relaxed state, and to open up to visualizing, imagining and creating healthy choices.

- I am going to be fine, and I am getting stronger all the time.
- I will repeat these affirmations to myself each day this week and continue as needed to incorporate them in my daily life.

When you're ready, return to your activities with renewed vitality and appreciation for yourself, knowing that you are in profound transition with many exciting possibilities. The first step is to believe it. Let yourself believe it.

(Suggested minimum time: 20 to 30 minutes.)

III. *Intimacy & Loss* ᖋ

*"It's the heart afraid of breaking
that never learns to dance.
It's the dream afraid of waking
That never takes the chance."*
—Amanda McBroom[6]

When I started up with Winter, I wanted to dance. Something in me wanted to awaken…a dream of intimacy, shared joy, ecstasy. I wanted to know myself more deeply. I opened up to love in ways I had not dared before. There was an inner spiritual drive to bond that I was trusting and following. She joined me in this soul-awakening dance.

Blessed is that union of two hearts rejoicing in ways that transcends the individual expression of joy. It is the dance which celebrates the culmination of the lifelong search for a soul mate. This drive to mate is essential in all life forms, animals and plants alike; it is in life's genetic code for the very survival of the species. It is more than genetic, it is an existential quest to become more fully human. This drive for intimacy comes from our inner knowing that there is more in life to be experienced in union with a mate than we can know in our aloneness. It is the desire to actualize and to complete ourselves. It is as natural an unfolding of our soul as the bending of plants toward the sun as they come to flower. This quest is our spiritual journey, and love is our most complete expression of ourselves in relationship. We seek love to experience our lives more fully.

The power for our bonding quest is also fueled by our drive to avoid the psychic pain experienced in loneliness. Loneliness is the dark side of the intimacy we seek. We all need alone time to reflect on our inner life, and to find our meaning and purpose, but none of us really wants to be lonely. Loneliness cries out saying:

> *I want to be involved in life's activities, with*
> *an intimate partner. I long to share my life with*
> *another person.*

The Dance Toward Unity

There are stages of development in all relationships. The excitement of meeting an attractive person and feeling their attraction to you is one of the most vibrant experiences we can have. Even in these early stages, it is not just poetic to say that there is "good chemistry" happening between two people. There is in fact powerful chemical activity going on as our emotions trigger a deep and ancient echo for spiritual bonding. Physical attraction is the seed power for a developing relationship. This drive for unity is more than just a sexual or sensual experience, although these senses are primary and necessary for the deeper spiritual love that can develop. Intimacy can emerge quickly in the early stages of exploring, and there is a great shared joy in the sense of possibility that something wonderful (full of wonder) is happening. We call this "falling in love" and our sense of falling is because we abandon any holding back of our trusting and hoping. We dismiss all the guards who carry the armor protecting our hearts.

It is interesting that the heart is such a universal symbol of romantic love. It is because the heart is recognized as the source of life force. Joy, ecstasy, and peace are all heart-felt experiences, and are known more fully in our most intimate moments with our mates. Within these feelings lies the sense of unity we have longed for since our first awareness of being alone in the world.

This mated bliss provides a more dimensional and textured

experience than we can know individually. This feeling has a certain ethereal quality to it which can't really be explained in scientific or logical ways. It is best captured by the poets and the songwriters of every generation. My attempt to display such a wondrous human event in the following chart is feeble in terms of all the fullness that is unexpressed, but I hope it will let you see that relationships develop with movement and qualities nurtured by both partners. As in all life, the desire is for an unfolding in time toward fullness.

SEVEN STAGES OF INTIMACY

Attraction & Exploration	Beginning serious relationship possibilities.
Steady Dating with Discovery & Friendship	Getting to know the other person.
Building a Foundation For Relationship	Liking what you find out.
Opening to Commitment	Daring to dream.
Expectation for a Life Together	Sharing that dream.
Love with Commitment	Being there in good times and hard times with support and joy.
Deep Spiritual Bonded Love; A Feeling of Unity	Shared wonder, ecstasy, and bliss.

In the song, *The Rose*, by Amanda McBroom, the message is that you cannot fully experience the dance if you are afraid of breaking your heart. The dream does not awaken without the dreamer taking the chance. If you don't take the chance, it's probably because a) you don't trust that your love will be reciprocated, and b) you are not trusting yourself to know that you can survive even if your love is not returned in full.

To trust yourself to let go to love requires an inner knowing that you can give yourself fully to another person, survive intact, and be no less if the other person chooses not to stay in the relationship. It is knowing that your life will be richer because of the giving of yourself. The truth is you can't really have your full self unless you are willing to give yourself fully. To hold back on letting go to love is to let some part of your spiritual life die or be locked away.

When couples are spiritually bonded, there are elements from all the other levels. Attraction, discovery, and commitment need to remain on-going and renewable as part of the dance between partners. Being in this spiritually bonded love is an intensely joyful state. It is also a time of great vulnerability because so much of your identity is in context with another person.

Because love needs to be nurtured, courtship behaviors such as being attractive and thoughtful should continue. It means the giving of flowers and special cards or "silly" gifts to carry the "I love you" message in fresh ways. Dating each other and taking time to go out to dinner, to go dancing, to take a walk, or catch a movie is essential in maintaining vitality in love. Couples need to take weekends away and other extended holidays when they can arrange it. The message in all this is:

> *I care for you, am attracted to you, want to be with you, treasure our love, and don't take you for granted. I want to explore what it means and feels like to be fully human, fully alive, fully me, when I am with you.*

Another Piece of My Story

In my relationship with Winter, we grew in our love to experience this deep spiritual bond. It was a letting go into sharing a dream. It was a dance of mutuality, each of us giving and taking full measure. Our love was so alive with joy and a feeling of wholeness, that we both worked hard to nourish it and to try to maintain it in the face of life's other demands of jobs, friends, and family.

With this deeply committed love, we had an implicit understanding that our friendship was the foundation upon which our relationship was built. The core of our friendship was the joy of sharing our lives with a willingness to work together, to initiate, to accommodate, to compromise, and to support each other. There was an openness of communication where we each felt a sense of safety in sharing inner thoughts and feelings without being judged or criticized. I felt totally accepted as a person.

Winter and I rejoiced in this deep spiritual bond of love for the better part of six years. That is not to say that we didn't have issues which came up; we did, and we dealt with them as directly and as lovingly as possible. For the most part, when Winter and I were together, there was this blissful state of flowing much like in a dance when you feel no hitches. There was no efforting and no self-consciousness. Once we were dancing in the kitchen to music on the radio, the music stopped but we continued dancing to our own inner rhythms for some time before we realized that we were dancing to the news broadcast. We had a raucous laugh and returned to preparing our meal. We were so delighted in the joy of our life and in each others company, that such activities as grocery shopping and preparing a meal were great fun. It was this optimism of feeling good and realizing we were able to create this good feeling that pulled us together. It was a joining of our spirits which created a strong element of reverence for our bounty.

We both happened to be very positive and optimistic people, and it was this notion of "sunshine faith" that served to sustain us when we were apart and in facing any difficult times. Before we were living together, we fell easily into a pattern of making contact every day by phone or mail. This communication was extremely reassuring and nurturing. Always the message was: "I miss you, am here for you, and am eager to be with you to celebrate our love."

Falling from Grace

What happened? How does such a spiritually-bounded love fade? It's a huge question, and it needs to be answered if there is to be healing. Because it is enormous and complex, this question will be dealt with extensively in Chapter Nine when I talk about the need to understand.

In every relationship, you will at times experience stress as individual personal issues inevitably arise. In these stressful times, the mated dance won't hold the familiar intensity and harmony, and you will feel somewhat off-center when these differences are experienced beyond a reasonable amount of time.

When Winter and I decided to move in together, we were, to some extent, able to predict that what was coming down the pike, was not going to be at all easy.

- The legal paperwork on my divorce was not finalized.
- My four sons were a continuing high priority for me.
- Winter's perceived role as a "stepmother" was one in which she felt at best ambivalent, and only marginally accepted, since my sons' affections and loyalties were clearly with their mother.
- In addition, Winter was choosing to give up her career and her house when she moved in with me.

Even with these dark clouds looming, some of which were visible, we moved in together with cautious optimism. I had idealized our relationship so much that I created a fairy tale where magic solutions to big problems would come just in time to save the hero and heroine. In reality, the transition was less than smooth and my heroic fantasy was not unfolding quite as ideally as I had imagined.

We had both invested in building a house which I was contracting. What with that, working full-time, trying to be a good partner with Winter, and a good parent to my sons, I was stressed. I just kept telling myself that as soon as the house was built, we would move in, and, like the rest of the fairy tale I was living in…live happily ever after.

When we didn't make love our first night in our new home, I remember telling myself that these things would all be better as soon as we settled in. It's marvelous how these little self-assurance rationalizations worked to protect me from the pain I wouldn't face. Making love had always been a part of our celebration. The house represented our nest, and its completion signaled that we were a significant step closer to "our" dream. When we were not able to fully celebrate when we moved in, the seeds of doubt were sown in my head. It was a clear signal that this nest was fulfilling my dream...not hers. I had been so focused on keeping my life together and the construction rolling, that I didn't want to dwell on the signals which Winter had been giving for many weeks trying to let me know that she had doubts about "our" dream. I felt that to get into her doubts would have taken me right out of the momentum of establishing our new home.

In retrospect, I can see that the signs of Winter's and my not making it were everywhere around me with critical comments and doubts replacing assurances. My denial system was so ingrained as a functional part of my optimism, that I successfully avoided facing this harsh reality for several months. I had dismissed her emerging depression and mood swings as due to her career quandary, and the loss she was feeling from having given up a job where she had been a nationally recognized leader in her field. It was our sixth summer, and we had been living together for just over a year.

I had arranged to teach in Colorado and our initial plan was that Winter would join me for six weeks of summer travel and holiday with my two younger sons, John and Chris. At the last minute, an opportunity came up for Winter to fill in as an interim director of a family-planning agency. She elected to remain at home and to join me later in Vancouver for the last leg of the trip home across Canada. We were apart for four weeks—the longest stretch of time we had experienced away from each other since we had met almost six years earlier.

In our first days apart, she wanted me to call her often. I

liked the idea, it made me feel needed and cared about. After only a couple of weeks, I felt a different tone emerging from her as we spoke long-distance over the telephone.

The Shock of Getting the News

Our time away had proven to be an opportunity for Winter to make the break, a decision that I suspect was painful, confusing, and no doubt in some ways exciting for her. She was opening up to new possibilities and that also meant new relationships.

I got the news over the telephone:

> *I've been growing in new directions. I am enjoying*
> *my time alone. I've been spending some time with a*
> *new friend. He's very intelligent and athletic and....*

I had to sit down and try to get myself together. I was absolutely stunned! Shaken to the core! I was visiting my brother and his wife, and Winter was coming in two days to meet them for the first time. I wanted them to like her. I told myself that everything would be okay when she got there, and she could feel my love and the joy of our relationship.

Waiting for her for the next two days was a nightmare for me. I was facing the dilemma of breaking down and telling my brother my worst fears, and afraid that if I did, it might contaminate his opinion of the woman with whom I was planning to share the rest of my life. My pain was amplified because I was choosing not to share it with anyone.

I didn't think John and Chris would understand, or maybe I thought it would only make them have more hope that I would get back together with their mother. In any case, I felt too afraid, stupid, and confused to let my feelings out. Mostly, I felt incredibly sad and tried to mask it all.

I kept up the facade until Winter and I had time to be together and figure out what we were going to do. She came to Vancouver, and we pretended to ourselves and to others that all was well. For the moment, I rationalized that all we needed was time together to sort it all out. Our trip across Canada with John and Chris was a mixture of joy with intermittent anxiety as I sensed that all was not well between us. Winter had changed, and as we settled in at home, the struggle to work things out became all consuming. After several weeks it became clear that she wanted to move out. It was November. I felt as cold and bare as the trees facing a New Hampshire winter.

The Bigger the Love the Harder the Fall

Our love had been like a giant sequoia to me, and when that tree fell, the ground on which I stood shook me to the core. It is clear that the more deeply your love has developed, the greater will be your loss if the relationship breaks up. If you have held back, and not let yourself feel deeply, or if your love was simply in the early stages of development, the pain from the loss is just not as great. The following chart demonstrates my guess at what people might experience in losing a relationship at various stages of development.

STAGES OF INTIMACY	LEVELS OF LOSS
Attraction & Exploration	Confused
Steady Dating	Concerned
Developing Foundations for a Lasting Relationship	Upset and disappointed
Openness to Commitment	Deeply hurt
Love with Expectation	Loss of trust; feeling betrayed
Love with Commitment	Loss of a dream
Spiritual Bond	Devastated

When Winter left, it felt to me like a dam had broken. I was flooded with feelings and experienced the whole range of trauma levels from confusion to devastation. The major circuits and connections to my world had been blown. My relationship with Winter was the platform on which rested my dreams, hopes, and sense of fulfillment.

I was in shock and disbelief, and that was just the tip of the iceberg. The loss of my dream, the loss of my hope, and the loss of my trust flew in the face of my optimistic view of life. My world view would need to be adjusted to assimilate such devastation. Easy to say—not so easy to do!

One could argue that I should not have invested so much in my relationship with Winter and thus been able to avoid my vulnerability, and the pain I experienced when she left. That channel is open for me to hear, but the stronger signal in me says:

> *I can only know such love by daring to dream and by abandoning those anchor points which hold me back. I choose to share deeply and intimately with another person.*

How is it that I could love Winter after she left? I had just lost the love of my life (so I felt at the time). I was incredibly sad and grieving, and something in me felt love for her even as she left and gave up on us. In the beginning, my motivation was not wanting to burn any bridges. I hoped Winter would come to her senses and remember what a fantastic, adoring, forgiving, stable man I am, and return to the joy we shared.

When she couldn't return, I felt amazed, and full of disbelief. It never occurred to me that she was doing anything more than trying to find herself in only a temporary quandary. I thought this would be easy. I did not feel betrayed; I just felt that she was lost. It was as if she had just wandered off, and I thought she would be back (Joe optimist).

> *In time, I was able to see that she wasn't coming back.*

It's not that it was easy to let go of the beautiful bond we shared; I made it clear that I wanted her to stay. I also knew that if she had to leave, nothing I could do would hold her. Since I still cared for her deeply, I could wish for her the best of whatever, whenever, and with whomever. I didn't want any less for myself.

Affirmation

> *I am willing to explore the possibility that I can love my leaver, knowing that when I can find this love that I will be less burdened. Bitterness is a burden and festers. Love heals. I will let go to love.*

Repeat this each day this week, and post it on your refrigerator, your bathroom mirror or both.

IV. Fake It 'till You Make It: Uses & Abuses of Denial ✍

Denial allows us to pretend to be strong while we go about coping with the rest of the world. To allow the full force of our devastation into consciousness is to run the risk of falling apart and losing it all together.

Denial is the First Defense

Denial worked like an automatic pilot to soften the impact and enable me to deal with the shock and disbelief I was experiencing.

She'll be back.
This is just temporary.
Hold on, give it another chance.
Wait and see.

At some level I knew I had been devastated; that my dream had been shattered. My body wisdom took over, calling upon denial to slow down the pain. Another word for body wisdom is intuition, and it's what Krishnamurti[7] calls our highest level of intelligence. It is when the whole of our experience, perception, memory, emotion, intellect, spirit and bodily sensing all come together to signal that we can trust our judgment.

Denial is that part of the wisdom which says: Don't burn any bridges; maybe things will work out." It was important to only gradually admit that things between Winter and me were not just great. Pretending helped me save face and keep hope alive.

As the first defense mechanism[8] in our protective armor, denial plays on any uncertainty and favors looking on the brighter side of maybe. To look on the darker side is more pain than you can deal with in the moment. In my relationship with Winter, my trust was complete. I had abandoned any self-protective mechanisms which would limit involvement with her. When the sword came down, I was the wounded knight, and quickly restored my armor in the "maybe" of denial, and the hope that things might just work out. Finding reasons to believe that, and holding onto even the slightest hope was part of my psychological adaptation. It helped me to keep going.

In these early stages of my denial, I said to myself

> *Everything will be okay as soon as the house is built. It will all work out as soon as she gets a job. She will come to her senses and come back to me. Just be patient and understanding.*

Denial is the guard at the switch who decides how much bad news to believe on any given day. You only let in what you can take.

Internal Dialogues

It wasn't just denial, a mixture of messages played in my head:

Sad Voice:	*I am feeling hurt, angry, stunned, confused, fearful, lonely and very, very sad.*
Coping Voice:	*Better find some support people.*
Doubting Voice:	*I wonder if there is something wrong with me? I feel exposed, and embarrassed. What went wrong? How could this greatest love of all time cease to be? Am I a jerk and don't know it? How could this happen to me? How could she give up all this adoration?*

Hopeful Voice: *Maybe we'll have a chance at rec-*
                                       onciliation.

Another Coping Voice: *Just keep control; it's too embar-*
                                         rassing to lose it! Shut up and go
                                         to sleep!

I was learning that I needed to listen to all these inner voices and find my balance.

A Note on Voices

It isn't that you actually hear the sound of voices, it's that we have taken in messages from our experiences which repre-sent a wide range of feelings and thoughts. These voices are what we imagine others might think or say. We have taken these voices in during our growing-up process, and we con-tinue to carry these messages with us into adult life as part of our identity. They help us define ourselves in terms of the way we should act if we are to be accepted in a particular culture or group. We get strong voices from specific cultural sub-stations such as the church, our parents, our current family members, the police, our neighbors, our peers, and our friends. These groups represent people or institutions whose messages are very familiar to us, even to the point of being stereotyped and generalized. They also represent established traditions and values which define acceptable manners, mores, and belief systems. Many people in our cul-ture live their lives very closely adhering to these "outside voices." To some extent we all want to please others and to gain the approval of, or to look good, in the face of real and imagined judges. We want to save face; we want to be a member of our group, of our family, and of our larger com-munity. We have a strong need to belong; it is how we find many of our satisfactions, and meanings in life. We choose to shape much of our behavior according to the strength of these outer voices.

Some typical outer voice messages from our culture that get into our heads are injunctions like:

- try hard
- be good
- be responsible
- be prompt
- honor your elders
- don't be taken advantage of

For boys there are special messages like:

- don't cry
- be strong
- be cool
- don't back down

And for girls:

- be nice
- be attractive, but not too
- don't flirt too much, nice girls are not too sexy

All of these messages from our various substations, play into our lives. It is not possible to shut out all the "shoulds" and "ought to's," but we can choose what we listen to and what we act on. The denial guard decides what to believe and what messages to let in. We learn that it may help us to pretend to be stronger than we actually may feel.

Whistling in the Dark: Pretending to Be Brave

We have all heard of the idea of "whistling in the dark." Because fear of the dark is universal and ancient, a powerful myth has been handed down to teach children to face their fear of the dark by whistling, pretending to be brave. The idea is that if you whistle you will be signaling to the ghosts, monsters, and demons that you are confident, strong, and not afraid. This simple act is a way of claiming power rather than giving it away. Even though you are afraid and unsure of yourself in the beginning, the whistling convinces you that you are just fine. Once you are through the dark passage, you in fact feel stronger and more confident. To not go into the darkness means you just don't get to the other side. You don't want to face your loss, but you have to. Facing your fear and acting confident brings you success in pushing yourself through to the light. While your intention was to pretend, you actually created a condition of strength by your pretentious behavior. Deciding to act, overrides unsubstantiated fear. We learn early on that it is okay to "Fake it 'till you make it."

Pretense is a natural defense which we have learned over evolutionary time. It is now built in to our genetic and cultural codes for survival. We have learned from our cave-dwelling heritage that bravado pays off. Bravado sustains and elevates our status, or it diminishes the status of peers through intimidation. To be perceived as weak is to be lower on the pecking order, and just as it is in the animal kingdom, there will be "picking on" and domination. Strength, or the appearance of it, has its privileges. Men have grown up in our culture feeling that it is particularly important to appear strong.[9] To admit a weakness or a loss might make us "lose face," and so we learn to deny and pretend.

The amazing thing is that, as you convince others of your strength, you also convince yourself. You become a model to yourself for the way you want to become. In time, you essentially move into the script of your pretended model. Although it may be a mask at first, acting stronger than you feel, will have the effect of making you feel stronger. Actions cause feelings to change just as feelings cause actions to change.

Uses of Denial

- Denial keeps hope alive.
- Denial helps keep things in the maybe and out of the absolute.
- Denial holds off the full impact of feeling devastated from the loss.
- Denial serves us in a transition period as we fight for stability, and to maintain our self-esteem.

- Denial feeds on even the slightest cues which support and reinforce what we want to believe.

For example:

She didn't say she wouldn't be back.

While this is a pretty thin cue, in the denial stage it is enough to hold on to for the moment.

Denial is a process which moves from a position near one pole of absolute refusal to believe the worst (that the relationship is lost), through a tentative position of (maybe the relationship is not lost), and on to admitting the truth of the outcome whatever it is. This movement is particularly important because denial must come to terms with the unfolding of reality.

Balance Principles of Denial

In order for denial to serve us in these useful ways, there needs to be a balanced perspective which will guard against rigidity.

It's tentative. Denial is healthy and adaptive as long as it's not carried to such an extent that we fail to face the truth and our pain associated with the outcome.

It gradually lets go. Denial serves us like the handle of a faucet, letting in reality and the truth of our feelings only at the rate at which we can stand the pain and still function. Sometimes that's just a trickle. When our dreams and the daily context of our lives are shattered by loss, there is a tendency to hold on to the past.

Abuses of Denial

Holding on to hope too long. A woman that I see for counseling (I'll call her Andrea) has continued to hold the torch for a man that left her five years ago. He occasionally calls and makes contact with her which is just enough to keep a faint hope alive for her (she stays hooked). Her identity is so caught up in her past partnership with him that she is having diffi-

culty seeing herself moving into another more healthy relationship. Andrea is settling for crumbs and hates herself for it.
She was so devastated when they separated that she did not
have enough self-esteem to "cut the cord." She is stuck in
denial. Even though he has been in other relationships over
the years, she refuses to believe that he won't be back.

This pattern for Andrea goes back to her childhood and her
dysfunctional family. Andrea felt abandoned at an early age,
when her father left home. She never really dealt with her hurt
and angry feelings about that loss. She felt that to do so would
only rock the boat and make things worse for her with her
mom, her stepdad, and with her real father. She learned to
"walk on eggs" around her parents. She learned to deny and
to suppress her feelings.

Andrea's case is not an isolated or uncommon experience in
our culture. Denial and suppression have been learned as a
way of remaining safe from anger, sadness, further abuse, and
possible abandonment.

The amount of time that you hold on to hope, and your
own particular way of denying, depends on the circumstances
of your relationship. Each of us will hold on for some period
of adjustment. There is no precise rule of thumb, but in
Andrea's case, she knows it has been too long. She has taken
herself into therapy to work it through.*

In my own case, I held on to hope for about seven months
(August–March). There were lots of signals from Winter that
suggested we might get back together. We saw each other often
throughout the fall, and spent New Year's Eve together. Even as
late as February, when she came for dinner, I remember her asking herself out loud "Why did I ever leave?" In some ways, I
was ready to take her back because I was missing her so much,
but my spirits couldn't really soar because I sensed that she
wasn't really able to come back. It was clear that she was only

---

*It is satisfying to report that now, eight months later, Andrea has not only
let go, she is in a wonderful new relationship in which she experiences open
communication of feelings, mutual respect, and support.

voicing her confusion. I took it as a nostalgic reflection and an acknowledgement of our love, but I knew she wasn't really returning.

Rosy Distortion. This is when you paint such a rosy picture publicly, that you don't admit the possibility that your relationship is not going to work. It's when there is so much denial that you embellish and distort stories which support the image you're trying to project.

> **Colleague:** "How's it going, Dwight?"
>
> **Dwight:** "Great! Winter is taking some time out, but we're still close and seeing each other. I'm hopeful that we'll work it out."

The danger here is that in addition to the devastation of the loss which you have not let yourself admit or fully feel, you also run the risk of looking foolish and losing face with your friends and family when the failure of the relationship is evident to everyone. Losing face is to open yourself to ridicule, and can be a significant blow to your self-esteem.

I found that it was better for me to just be a bit vague:

> *I don't know what's coming down the road, it does not look great, but we're talking.*

Being vague and general allowed me to keep my pain somewhat more private, and I could put emphasis on what was positive, which was that we were talking. This kept my denial tentative. An inner voice said:

> *Don't make your situation sound overly optimistic you could end up with egg on your face.*

I was aware that a large part of my being vague and tentative was that I just didn't want to look too foolish or feel so vulnerable. I had a sense of how the story would end, but I didn't want to admit it. I was trying to save face without egg on it. Denial is obviously counterproductive if you carry it into your outer world by not coming to terms with what is real. The ultimate state of grace includes being honest with yourself and with others.

Denial As Part of the Process of Disengagement

Humans are simply not meant to "slam the door shut" on important relationships. Our psyches are just not made for such brutality. Abruptness flies in the face of caring, commitment, respect, understanding, and love. Disengagement needs to be a gradual process. Denial helps us to keep a sense of "maybe" and to hold on to a sense of meaning, context, and continuity.

It is our engagement with hope that fends off letting in the message of "It's over." We all know of couples who have had temporary breakups, then come back together, and felt stronger. It's what we want for ourselves. We can imagine it. We hope for it. We might even pray for it.

Being tentative and hopeful buys us time to sort through the chaos of our options. There are at least five reasons why we take time in disengaging from our most intimate partner.

- It serves us in coping with the crises of transition because we need to maintain stability in our daily functioning.
- Fundamentally, we don't want to hurt people we love, and so we avoid bluntness, attempting to communicate caringly, in the context of the love that is felt.
- We don't want to burn any possible bridges.
- It's not our nature to roll over and play dead.
- We need time to shape our images of what "It's over" means.
  - What's it going to look like?
  - How do we want it to be when it's over?
  - Will we still be friends?
  - Will I be able to be friends?
  - Will I want to?

 – Will I be hurt and angry?
 – How long is good-bye?
 – Is it forever, or is it "See you later"?
 – How much loss can I take?
 – How can I take this loss?

All these questions and more came to mind as I began to let reality in.

Holding on to hope with denial allows us to work through disengagement in a more gradual and gentle way.

Looking for Signals

During this disengagement time, we look for signals from our estranged partners. We keep our "maybe" alive for a long time in the following ways:

Amplifying any positive signals. Often I would get conflicting signals, and it was my nature to focus on the positive side of possibility. Some of the signals I tried to create, imagine, or look for in the flimsiest of experiences. For example: If Winter and I were going to have lunch and talk, I would imagine that this would be the day when she would come to her senses and decide to come back to me.

I took any sign of friendliness or warmth from her as a reinforcement of my belief that she would return to our committed love, and rebuild the bond we shared. I knew that such optimism wasn't well-founded, but hope overrides such rational circuits. Believing in these thin signals was just one more way of getting through the pain and postponing the blunt shock of finality.

Blocking negative signals. On other occasions, I simply would not let some negative signals in. For example: I might get an idea or an image of Winter and me not making it. I shut down that image. I feared it. Even though I knew that things were not right between us, I simply asked myself: "Who do I know that has everything all right?" or, kept telling myself: "Keep communicating...keep giving, not giving up"!

So I hung in there. Winter and I continued to talk, to grieve our loss together, and remained gentle with each other in keeping the signals tentative. This is what I call a drifting disengagement. It allows partners in the breakup to maintain some sense of balance and perspective in contrast to being blown away. There needs to be dialogue, understanding, and acknowledgement of the depth and beauty of the spiritual bond that was shared.

I found my beginning healing process to be somewhere between healthy denial (which allowed me to hold on to hope and possible bargaining) and the gradual acceptance of my pain. Somehow this denial and hope helped me to feel stronger, and able to talk more freely about my experience when I was with friends.

Coming Out of Denial: Talk Heals

As I began to let go of denial, I could gradually let in reality and listen to a chorus of survival voices going on in my head. In the beginning there were two very clear tones:

Coping Voice: *I am tough and capable: I can hide my hurt and pretend I am just fine. This will keep me functioning and I can cope with my job and my other relationships.*

Feeling Voice: *I'm feeling alone, sad, confused, angry, hurt and depressed. I need to be with someone. I need to talk, to share my burden and to sort through this chaos.*

Coping Voice: *If I talk about my pain I will bore people and they won't want me around much. They might be afraid of my pain and let my depression take them down. I'd better keep my mouth shut.*

Feeling Voice: *I have a big ache and it won't go away.*

Coping Voice: *I still have to cope so I will let the pain in a lit-*
                    tle at a time. I'll get over it; it's just going to
                    take time.

I needed and wanted to share my troubles and confusion
with friends and family. I also didn't want to carry on a pretense or avoid contact with people that I trusted to understand
and care. Sharing with others helped me sort out my feelings so
that I could try to make some sense out of what had happened.

My two best men friends, Ben and David, came for lunch
one day, and I took the opportunity to share my grief and confusion with them. I thought out loud:

> *How could she not want all this adoration. I don't*
> *think I'm too smothering. She can do her own*
> *thing and it's fine with me, as long as she doesn't*
> *have sex with anyone else.*

(For me, our sexual intimacy was sacred ground and an
important part of our spiritual bond.)

I remember a tingling sensation in my nose as I fought back
tears and tried to mask my feelings with humor:

> *And besides, how could she not love me, I'm such*
> *a great guy.*

I laughed at myself with them even as tears filled my eyes.
This was an important time of sharing and helped ease the
sadness and embarrassment I was feeling. Picking up the invitation to keep it light, they would chide me saying:

> *Right Dwight. You're such a great guy, how could*
> *she do this?*

It let me know they cared and that I could go on at my own
pace.

It helps me to feel better if I can laugh at myself when I
have looked a little foolish. Adding the lightness of humor
unloads the impact of the insult.[10] Humor means that at some

level you can stand back and see yourself, accept your denial process, and see that it's okay; you're just getting through it in the best way that you can.

I knew I didn't want to go on and on with David and Ben about this gloom I was feeling. As it turned out, I didn't really need to. A few minutes of sharing allowed me to get centered. It is natural to be off-center and out of balance when there is trauma. It is pain signaling to get my attention. Once the pain was out, I felt immediately better, and able to relate with them on other issues.

Fortunately, neither Ben nor David were the kind of people to offer advice or solutions. I remember once wanting to get reassurance and I asked them: "Do you think she will come back?" I didn't like Ben's response. He said: "I think you know the answer to that question."

The truth of his comment was a little chilling. I was at first embarrassed, then angry and defensive as I stammered "What do you mean?" I knew what he meant, knew he was right, and didn't like the pain which the truth was causing me.

I found family members and other friends with whom I could share some of my pain and confusion, including my four sons, David, Michael, John, and Chris. Being open with them has been an important part of the foundation of our love which has remained strong. Lines of communication remain open when there are no taboo topics to avoid. Sharing with others was not so much wanting to disperse the load as much as it was that I wanted to be congruent in my relationships. Congruent is a great word to express wholeness. When I am congruent, I am all in one piece, and what I am saying fits with how I am feeling and how I am behaving. This concept is so well put forward in the writings of Carl Rogers,[11] I recommend him to all readers.

It became clear that being comfortable enough to talk about my dilemmas with others was my first step out of denial. To remain alone and closed off from sharing with others was just too lonely. Intuitively, I knew that I needed to face my feelings and share with those closest to me. Opening up to talk was an important example of my acting on my intuition. The payoff was great, I felt accepted, understood, and cared about. It was the beginning of lightening my load.

I feel strongly that being open and sharing personal issues with friends is what friendship is all about. It is a first step in taking care of myself. For me to open deeply to my most personal feelings and struggles, opens the door for others to be real with me, and to share their vulnerabilities should the need arise for them.

If friends or family are not available for you at this time, it would be important to take yourself into counseling to get through denial, and to get on with the important process of grieving and healing. Accepting that you have this need to grieve is a fundamental part of loving yourself and the foundation for loving your leaver.

Other Coping Mechanisms

Although denial captures the essence of a particular stage in grieving, there are many other coping mechanisms which support denial and your ability to deal with the pain of your loss.

For example, the chart opposite demonstrates three other coping mechanisms and strategies (self-talk) aimed at specific outcomes (desired effect).

It's important that you understand that being rejected is a primary assault on your sense of self, and our first response to rejection is a survival response. I think the use of the word mechanism in describing these systems of self-support is quite appropriate because it all happens quite automatically. These coping mechanisms are built into our genetic structure and are reinforced in life as we experience the surviving of psychological assault.

Our coping mechanisms are honed to a fine edge. They are subtle and they are unconscious. They come into focus and perform just when they need to. Today I may need to deny, and

COPING MECHANISM	SELF-TALK	DESIRED EFFECT
Denial:	*I'll hang in there because this can't really be happening to me. It will all work out.*	Keeping hope alive.
Rationalization:	*We didn't really have a match anyway; she's not the one for me.* (sourgrapes!) or *I'll like being single.* (sweet lemon)	Discounting and diminishing the importance of your experience together.
Generalization:	*They're all like that.*	Trying to create distance.
Reflection:	*What the hell happened?*	Reduce bewilderment
	Why did I invest myself in this relationship?	Awareness

tomorrow I may need to ventilate my hurt and frustration.

I discovered that my coping mechanisms were well-intact to serve me. My job was to see that they didn't over-serve me by keeping me stuck in denial, rationalization and so on.

We use these mechanisms quite automatically. The boundaries between these defenses are not crisp and well-defined as we move from one to another, surviving emotional conflict. Our particular defenses depend on the context of our relationship, our feelings, and the level of hope we have on any given day in our grieving process. For example: I may be feeling "It's all going to work out," (denial) and in the next moment I may be wondering "What the hell happened?" (reflection).

As I began to lose hope, I began creating more distance by discounting (rationalization and generalization) my relationship and my feelings about the loss.

I found that asking myself questions helped me keep things in perspective, even though I would not always get an immediate answer. Just the asking would help me focus on what I needed to learn.

> *What happened?*
> *How did I set this up this way?*
> *What do I need to do now?*
> *Is it possible to turn this separation around?*
> *Can we still be friends?*
> *When will I ever feel better?*

Questions to myself and thoughts to myself, and more questions, and more thoughts...until I sorted through the chaos. These reflective questions were the soul wrenching dilemmas of my search for inner peace. They represented the heart of my energy for balance and clarity. Self-exploration was the pump that kept my grieving process circulating.

I was looking for the light at the end of the tunnel. Reflecting and questioning were my search lights in the darkness. I kept looking for the brighter way down the path, I wanted out of that dark place.

I have a new way of seeing and interpreting that old saying "Light at the end of the tunnel." I have come to see that the light at the end of the tunnel is a reflection of my own search-light. I want to believe the light is there, and so I see it, or imagine it, as I look ahead.

SUGGESTED ASSIGNMENTS

I. Exploring denial voices in your journal.

Take time for yourself and listen for your inner messages of denial. There will likely be several voices. Let this be a rich, free-flowing dialogue. These voices will all have something to say about sex, anger, blaming, healing, becoming vulnerable, pretending, and so on. Give full expression to each voice that wants to be heard. Try to keep your journal daily or as often as is "write for you."

II. Ten Good Ideas

Below are listed the five things to do and five things to avoid. Start today by trying to practice all the behaviors which promote the healing process, and avoid any of the attitudes or behaviors which block the healing process.

CHOICES & ATTITUDES WHICH PROMOTE HEALING	CHOICES & ATTITUDES WHICH BLOCK THE HEALING PROCESS
Things To Do:	**Things To Avoid:**
• Know that denial is part of the healing process, and listen to all the inner voices as you find your balance. Trust your intuition to face the truth at your own pace as you cope and get stronger.	• Remaining stuck in denial, pretending that everything is okay with you.

- Value your experience by acknowledging the caring and love you once shared. Admit the depth of your love and your loss.

- Devaluing your experience by continuing to discount your love in order to make it seem unimportant.

- Share your feelings and vulnerabilities with friends with whom you feel safe and accepted.

- Acting so tough and invulnerable that you "go it alone." (This will not impress anyone that matters to you in the long run.)

- Be gentle and patient with yourself, seeing healing as a process.

- Jumping to conclusions and burning bridges with your former mate.

- Keep searching and sorting to find the light at end of tunnel.

- Giving up.

V. Harboring Ill Feelings: Anger Wounds the Carrier ✍

It is interesting that in our culture, we use the expression "harbor ill feelings." Harboring anger keeps you anchored in anger. It is a trap. If you hold on to anger, it will surely stay with you. We make ourselves ill when we harbor ill feelings.[12]

Holding on to resentment is not only an immediate burden for you, it will have serious effects on your physical, social, psychological, spiritual and sexual life. We are whole, integrated beings. Harboring anger and resentment is holding on to toxic waste in your system, and will make you ill or ill-tempered or both!

The Blame Game

If I blame another person or an event for what has happened to me, I am to some extent failing to take responsibility for my own life. Blaming seeks a simple answer to a complex situation. Many people may blame themselves, but this too may be a refusal to see the complexity and the context of the circumstances and the relationship. If we lock into blame, we bypass our other feelings, and cannot complete the grieving and healing process. Blame by definition does not heal. As long as you continue to blame, you have not let go. The more bitterness and anger we carry around—the more bitter and angry we become. Angry, hurtful interactions with your former mate only serve to keep you from healing. There is nothing gained in holding on to anger and resentment. Blaming will only stop when you can stand back and see yourself and ask: "What is this anger all about?"

Anger: The Mask That Hides Our Inner Feelings

When I feel angry, I know it's because I am either hurt or afraid, or both. If I am able to admit these primary feelings to myself, my anger does not dominate my consciousness nor my behavior. If I don't see the hurt and fear (or rather won't let these feelings in), the danger is that these feelings will be covered over and masked by anger.

Our culture does not acknowledge hurt and fear as being as honorable as anger. Admitting that you are hurt and feeling fearful or doubting, means being vulnerable, and by definition this status is not perceived as a safe place except for the very secure person. Men in particular are conditioned in our culture to be invulnerable, to be macho, and not to express hurt and fear. Anger, and the pretense of invulnerability, are more acceptable, even respected and admired in some circumstances. I'm reminded of a poem by my friend Gay Hendricks. He captured something of this macho-dilemma when he wrote the following:

Taking Out Some Aggressions
On Aging Western and War Heroes
God damn you, John Wayne
I wish you hadn't taught me to swagger
And
Shoot from the hip.
You too, Jeff Chandler,
You kept your cool,
And I kept my cool, too.
I submerged a lot of feeling because of you, Audie Murphy.
A lot of perceptions went down the drain

Between twelve and twenty.
I didn't become a man until I learned not to act like one.
You won the West and a couple of wars with your
invulnerability.
It took me only twenty-one years and two ruined
love affairs to learn that Invulnerability
can
Kill you.
—*Gay Hendricks*[13]

It's not just men. Most people bypass admitting that they are hurt or afraid, and just get angry or defensive. It's what we learn in our families and our culture at large. Our first impulse is to get even, to hurt back, and attempt to regain some sense of control. I want you to know that behind the mask of anger, there are many hidden feelings which have been denied, feelings which may explode into overreaction, or stay buried and cause you much emotional pain and eventual physical distress.

Models in the Media

Movies and television are primary sensory experiences which impact our belief systems from early childhood. While there is concern and much written about the negative effects of all the violence which is displayed before us, the violence continues. Often the most popular films and TV shows suggest that it is not only "okay," but that it is good to be suspicious, argumentative, defensive, and to blame others for what happens to us. Revenge and retribution are acceptable norms in our society. Being angry is portrayed as being strong, even as heroic. We applaud John Wayne who stands up for himself with counter aggression; it creates drama in our lives, and echoes our more primitive instincts for justice. It does not make growing up in our culture an easy task, particularly when our heroes and heroines model the masking of their true underlying feelings of hurt and threat.

Anger: A Coat of Many Colors

It's not just hurt and fear that are behind anger, although these are the two primary feelings. The truth is that anger is an expression of a matrix of emotions and is related to a myriad of feelings and circumstances. Using the alphabet as a stimulus, it is not difficult to see the variety and interconnections of feelings which may be associated with anger:

A. Agitated, not amused.
B. Betrayed, belittled.
C. Confused and caring.
D. Disappointed, not delighted.
E. Emotional, not ecstatic.
F. Frustrated and fearful.
G. Ghastly, not good.
H. Hurt, and perhaps a little hopeless and helpless.
I. Ignored, and maybe a little ignorant.
J. Jealous, not jolly.
K. Not Kindly.
L. Lousy and lonely.
M. Maudlin.
N. Nostalgic and needy.
O. Overwhelmed not optimistic.
P. Pessimistic and perhaps panic.
Q. Queasy.
R. Rage.
S. Stunned and sad.
T. Tricked, tired, and tumultuous.
U. Upset and undone.
V. Vexed and vituperative.
W. Wasted.
X. eXtremely everything.
Y. Yearning for resolution.
Z. CraZy.

Of course, there are many more feelings than this which could accompany and fuel your anger. While this stream-of-consciousness-list is zany and superficial, it is useful to point out how feelings are so varied and so pervasive, with some being more in the foreground at any given moment. Our feelings are like the proverbial "Can of Worms." They are imbedded in the totality of our experience and personal history.

The point is not to deny anger, it is to understand all the feelings which surround and accompany it. To embrace the totality of your feelings in this way, is to acknowledge the depth and the breadth of your ability to experience life. Anger has its roots in deep caring and passion for life. We often sabotage access to those deeper feelings, by not looking beyond or beneath the steaming of our anger.

Feelings Always in a Mix

Feelings are never singular or isolated. Instead they accompany each other in complex interactive ways. For example, you may feel various levels of sadness, frustration, loneliness, anger, and fear washing over you within moments of each other. You may also feel quite confused about all of these and the many other feelings which get stirred up every time you think about or let yourself feel your loss. This confusion was a necessary state for me, serving to cloud much of the early stages of my grieving, and blocking the truths which hurt too much to let in. Confusion clouds and dulls the pain, and takes you into greater or lesser degrees of depression, to rest, and to sort out the chaos as you begin your healing.

Tunnel Vision: Getting Stuck in Anger

Many people find it very difficult to allow threatening feelings into consciousness. Such threat may make us feel more vulnerable than we want to tolerate. One way to avoid looking at, or dealing with pain, is to get angry and stay angry.

As I have pointed out, we are conditioned to respond with anger without looking at the hurt and fear, or at the caring and love.

Glen and Julie were in a marriage that wasn't working and she initiated the separation. He made a comment which struck me with resounding confusion when he said, "The only way I can get through this is to hold on to my anger."

I puzzled over this statement for a few days until it dawned on me how it was that this could work for Glen. By holding on to his anger, I could see that he didn't have to let himself experience the vulnerability of hurt, sadness, fear, confusion, and all of the other feelings associated with his loss. This kind of tunnel vision closes out the pain, as well as the opportunity for understanding and seeing the big picture.

When anger masks all the other feelings, the grieving process never gets completed. Like a washing machine with a faulty timer, your cycle may get stuck in anger. In one sense, anger is the ultimate escape for avoiding feelings. It serves to short-circuit your anxiety which gets stirred up with all your vulnerable feelings of hurt, fear, and self-doubt.

Holding on to anger also may help people to avoid having to deal with their fear of intimacy. Some people fear intimacy because they fear loss, rejection, and abandonment.[14] Their fear comes out unconsciously as anger, and their reasoning becomes: "If I stay angry, I can keep people from getting too close and then I won't get hurt again." It is a failure of trust, both of oneself and of others.

If you remain angry, you can have the illusion of control, as you try to become the rejector and not the rejectee.

Glen's response is not unique. Many people who have been previously hurt have held on to anger, and learned their patterns of avoidance at an early age. In Glen's case, he felt betrayed and stunned. He felt sad, embarrassed, and threatened, and could not face all these feelings. To avoid the overwhelming pain of all these, he chose anger to override and block his other feelings.

Anger As a Signal

When you are feeling angry, aggressive, abusive thoughts of revenge, it is important for you to know that this is a signal that you have been badly hurt, or are feeling very vulnerable. It is the hurt that needs to be looked at gently in a safe place with a safe person. This is an inward journey. Anger is an outward expression of surface energy from an untraveled inner road.

The first step then for dealing effectively with your anger is to see it as a signal, that something is going on beneath the surface. It is an opportunity to explore all of your associated feelings. For example, you might be feeling angry and discover that what is behind that anger is your fear of being alone. We all need and want to belong and to be in an intimate interdependent relationship. Aloneness may well provoke feelings of abandonment and questions of self-doubt such as: "Am I good enough to have a mate to love and to allow love into my life"? If you are feeling angry about your loss, it may be a signal to suggest that you look at the threat, the abandonment, the hurt, fear, and insecurity accompanying that anger.

To catch the signal and reflect on the message means you have to pause. The old clichés of "counting to ten" or "taking a few deep breaths" are in fact useful exercises to avoid impulsive "knee-jerk" responses to your anger. Our social evolution is gradually countering the tendency for the knee-jerk reaction of retribution. We are beginning to accept that it is not only appropriate to understand and experience our feelings, it is essential for healing.

We are privileged to be living in a time when there is a consciousness shift in our social evolution which is creating new norms of understanding and forgiveness as we enter the twenty-first century. We are discovering that we are capable of great love and compassion, which arises from a deep spiritual sense of knowing that this is our best way of being.[15]

Seeing the Big Picture

There is something in you that wants to make sense of the world. If you can get a handle on understanding how things happen, you are not as likely to repeat your mistakes. It is important to look at the history, the development, and the patterns of your relationship if you are to see the big picture of why you didn't make it as a couple. Any anger you may be feeling needs to be seen in the context of your total relationship. Anger also needs to be seen in the context of your total feelings and experience of yourself. How does your personal history figure into what's going on? Are there patterns which you are repeating? This big picture understanding will help you to dissipate your anger, because you begin to see the complexity of the other person, yourself, and the situation. When this happens, you find that you don't have to take things quite so personally.

In my own experience, I came to see that Winter was in an enormous transition in her life which included career change and plans to return to school for doctoral study. There were other matters:

- Family, do we want one?
- Money, how will it be shared and what are our spending priorities?

In any relationship there will be issues around individual personal development. There will be differences around values and attitudes with regard to sex, aesthetics, material possessions, and social ways of being, to point to only the more obvious. When we understand the context, we won't feel as angry because we won't take it as personally. The hurt will be less severe.

Seeing Yourself: Facing Your Feelings

The first days and weeks of my grieving, I was not interested in being psychological or analytical about my feelings, nor could I see the big picture that would unfold. It was only later that it gradually became clear to me that there were lots of ways in which I had been coping to get through my loss, and one of the things I realized was that I did not want to hold onto bitterness and blame.

After some weeks and months of my emotional pain and all the hundreds of feelings associated with my loss, I began to look back and notice that I was going through a process. I didn't feel the same in March as I had in November. I could see stages and specific experiences which had moved me through those stages. It was a slow unfolding.

I remember getting on a plane for Colorado when the idea for this book jumped into my head. It seemed to me that what I had been going through in my grieving was at least somewhat typical or similar to what others go through in relationship loss. I had been hurt, I had been down, and I knew I was healing, even though I couldn't see exactly where I was in my own "getting through it" or "getting over it" recovery process.

Looking at my own grieving put things in perspective for me; it interested me, and somehow standing back and looking at what I was doing and feeling, made me feel better. I began to write about my experience, first in a journal, and later by starting this book. This book is a direct outcome of my own experience with grieving and expresses feelings I discovered about myself as I wrote it.

I discovered that my feelings needed to be faced, each in their own time as I climbed out of my shock and disbelief. The principle I want you to learn here is:

> *To not face your feelings is to not complete your grieving.*

Resisting Feelings

Men are champions at resisting their feelings; we have been taught well from an early age.[16] Most men are uneasy about their sentimentality and tender feelings. We not only refuse

to admit our hurt and fear, we avoid exploring the whole
range of our feeling experiences. It is unsettling to open
these gates because our culture has told us that to be a man
is to be in control. Feelings do not want to be controlled;
they flow like water into the crevices of our pain, our playfulness, and our pleasure. Vulnerability lurks at every feeling
station and so we try to control the hurt. The problem is
that when we hold in our feelings, we become stuck or fixed
in denial, blame, or other defenses.

You may feel that a journey into your feelings is like an
excursion into the darkness of the night woods. I want to
show you that it is important to honor this fear and examine
this resistance and all your other feelings. It is the only way
through to healing. Feelings want to be felt, and part of that is
listening to the message of your feelings. The feelings will
always tell you what you need to do. You need to ask:

> *How does my anger serve me?*
> *What do I need to do to get through my depres-*
>   *sion?*
> *Is there a lesson to be learned in my frustration?*

I don't promise you that there are easy answers, solutions,
or overnight miracle cures for the pain of your loss, but these
questions will cause you unconsciously to begin to seek
answers. We must not shortcut our grieving experience by
denying or burying our feelings.

As someone who has been down the grieving path, I hope
that I can illuminate a path that will help you find your way
through your resistance and into awareness of your feelings,
your choices, and your deliberate behavior.

Trail Blazing

Because I do a fair amount of mountain and woods hiking, I
am always very grateful to those pathfinders who have gone
before, and have left a well-marked trail. Sometimes the bark

of trees is cut or painted in order to show me the next bend through woods when the best way is not always obvious. Above tree line, I find cairns of stones to point me in the right direction. These cuts, painted marks, or cairns are known as blazes on the trail. Thus the meaning of a trail blazer is that someone has been ahead of you and charted or mapped out a path through the territory. All of these thoughtful markers save me from the scratches of bushwackery, from detours which lead me astray, or worse yet from floundering lost into territory which seems unfriendly because it is unknown. Being lost is a terrifying experience. Going into the pain of your grief is a little like going into the woods. But the woods of your feelings do not have to have some hideous witch lurking behind an obscure thicket who will put you in the oven like Hansel and Gretel. Better to see the path than to leave bread crumbs as you journey ever so tentatively into your feelings. Bread crumbs represent your anchor point, your last safe known place in case you want to retreat. On this journey, you are going through the woods and not returning to your pain or to your old ways. They weren't working for you anyway. You are going to the top of the mountain and towards light. What you need is a path that is as well-lit and as well-marked as possible.

I believe it will be helpful for you if you can begin to see that you are somewhere in your own process of getting over your loss. I wrote this book to help you move through that process, and cycle upward to healing as quickly as possible.

Ask yourself these questions:

> *If I hold on to blame and anger, am I in someways being held hostage to these feelings which I direct outward?*

> *If I am an angry and bitter person am I really free?*

Anger, blaming, and bitterness will get in the way of healing. It will be helpful for you to see that you have choices around your emotions, and to know that there are healthy avenues to express your legitimate feelings.

Your feelings are the most immediate expression of your attempts to recover from the impact of your loss. Each one of your feelings holds a key to healing. Observe these feelings which are occuring in you, and know that to simply acknowledge them is the beginning of release, of understanding, and of healing.

VI. Moving Beyond Anger ↬

You need to believe that you are not stuck forever in your anger. Why hold onto it? Who is it hurting, but you? Let go of your anger and move on to a more peaceful and happy place.

The way out of your anger is to look within, and see what is going on for you. Here are some questions you might ask yourself.

> *How does my anger serve me?*
> *Does my anger keep me safe?*
> *Does my anger mask other feelings?*
> *What are my feelings?*

Just asking the questions will begin the process of discovery. Use your journal to write your feelings about these and other questions that come to you.

Your inner questions are important because without looking within, you will never fully understand your feelings. Understanding your feelings is the foundation for your health and vitality.

Your feelings are associated with everything you value. They are associated with your attitudes about every circumstance you encounter. They are the visceral part of your being, and represent a fundamental necessity for your personal growth. Let yourself feel.

Ask yourself other questions:

> *What is legitimate anger?*
> *Can I use the energy behind anger in a positive*
> *way?*
> *What are the dangers of anger?*
> *How might it backfire and destroy everything I*
> *really want?*

Your feelings are the key to helping you get through your hurt, your sense of threat and your sadness. This inward look will become an ongoing activity for you as you seek to continue to understand yourself. You eventually come to a point when you will ask yourself: "What do I need to do to express my anger in a healthy way and move through and beyond this pain and frustration?"

Legitimate Reasons to Be Angry

There are some very good reasons to be angry. It is appropriate to feel anger if you have been psychologically, physically, sexually, or spiritually abused. It is legitimate to be angry if another person expresses intentional malice toward us. I use three headings under which I understand legitimate anger in relationship loss.

Betrayal:	Your partner has been lying, cheating, or otherwise disregarding your feelings and breaking your trust.
Rejection:	Your partner has broken your commitment, has turned away and left you.
Domination:	There are many forms of domination. The following four headings summarize the major areas in relationship loss.
	Discounting. If a person that we care about makes a comment which somehow devalues

us, we don't like it. At some level, we all continually fight for self-respect. Part of how we know and respect ourselves comes from the messages we get from others on how we are valued. If we are discounted, it means the other person is being psychologically aggressive, and our feelings and needs are not considered.

Deciding things unilaterally. This means that you just don't figure into important decisions that affect the relationship. Your vote doesn't count.

Demanding things will go his/her way. This is a more aggressive form of the above. Not only does your partner not include you in the decision making, he or she demands that you accept the decisions without question or resistance.

Disregarding your feelings and needs. This would include the invasion of your privacy and the threatening of your personal security and well-being.

To have our physical or psychological space invaded by another person is a violation of our most basic needs for safety and survival. The invading may take obvious hostile forms such as hitting, unwanted sexual advances, and authoritarian verbal abuse, or less intrusive forms such as noxious noise or other thoughtless inconsiderations. We have a right to quiet places in our most personal living space. We have a right to safety and to peace.[17]

The truth is, we all want to be acknowledged, accepted, and prized by others. When we are not considered, we feel that we don't count for much. If we are ignored, we assume we have been judged in a negative way, and while we may not know why, we can imagine the worst. Such disregard means being rejected at our most heartfelt sense of who we are, and strikes at the heart of our most basic need to belong. When another person who is significant in our lives treats us this way, we are slighted by the imbalance of caring.

When any of these abusive acts impact on us, anger is our natural response which says: "I don't like being treated this way."

> **Principle:** Anger is always legitimate if you have been psychologically, physically, or verbally abused. Anger stems directly from intentionally hurtful acts.

Even as the above are legitimate reasons to be angry, it is still essential to look at all the underlying feelings which anger may hide. If you have been discounted and deceived, insulted, and ignored by your former partner, you have probably felt hurt, threatened, confused, sad, and frustrated. These feelings are the steam which is behind anger. Anger always has its roots in the energy of your underlying feelings. Be watchful of any over-reactions or distortions which contaminate your legitimate anger.

Healthy Expressions of Anger

Since it doesn't work to harbor anger, and blaming others only makes things worse, what do you do with these feelings? This is an important question, and the answer is complex. The obvious answer is to express all your feelings in healthy ways. But how? You have to ask: "What will create wellness? What are the healthy expressions of anger?" Getting through your anger in a healthy way is essential because if you don't get through it, you don't get well.

We have all been cooked in the cake of custom, and we have been conditioned by powerful cultural norms which reinforce aggression, revenge, and cold-shoulder approaches to problem solving. We have also been taught to stuff our feelings, stay quiet, and avoid rocking the boat. To break these patterns we need to see and experience healthy expressions of our anger. It is not easy to detach yourself from your well-worn and well-entrenched patterns. It will take hard work, continuing practice, and it will take time. The first step out of these worn out patterns is to accept that your feelings are yours, they are part of you, and they add the texture, tone, and vitality of your expression of yourself. Claim your own feelings, honor them, and try to understand them. To choose this path is to become more aware and to grow toward your own best way of being. As you make friends with the feelings behind your anger, you come to know that there are options for you beyond your usual patterned angry responses.

I use four general categories to frame my understanding of healthy expressions of anger.

Venting: Physical and emotional release to restore your balance.

Assertiveness: Claiming and expressing your legitimate feelings, needs and wants.

Rationalization: Maintaining your positive beliefs in hard times.

Rebuttals: Creating and sustaining your positive belief system.

Venting

Not all venting is healthy. The rule is: Venting is healthy if it is not at someone else's expense. Venting is damaging if it is abusive. Such things as "kicking the dog" or otherwise taking out your aggression on a subordinate being, or object, will not help in dealing with your anger. Guilt will come in and mediate your pleasure if it is at someone else's expense.

Some appropriate ways of venting are:
- talking out your feelings with a friend or counselor
- keeping a journal
- hitting pillows
- chopping wood
- running, or other sports workouts
- yelling

All these activities and others may be enormously helpful in releasing stressful tension in psychological and/or physical ways. The body wants balance and seeks it relentingly as hunger drives us toward food.

Assertiveness

In our culture, we are more often taught the extremes of either being aggressive and revengeful, or of being overly passive and allowing others to take advantage of us. In relationships,
- we need to take care of our own needs.
- we need to know that we deserve our share and not less.
- we need to stand up for our beliefs and our rights.

To be assertive is to claim our legitimate needs, and our right to be respected as we express ourselves to meet our basic needs. Assertiveness means that we can express our own feelings, values, and opinions with passion, clarity, and directness. We have a right to our feelings, and a responsibility to ourselves to express them in ways which do not infringe upon the rights of others.

"I" Messages

The first step for me in becoming more assertive and standing up for my rights and needs is to be in touch with what I am feeling. The more clear I am, the more I can claim the legitimacy of my feelings, and the less likely I will be to get into blaming.

I'm greatly indebted to Tom Gordon[18] for his work in "Effectiveness Training." His model of communication has been very important in my life. He talks about "I" messages as a way of owning and expressing our feelings by giving an objective non-blaming description of the act which causes the feelings.

A typical "I" message looks like this:

I am angry because you broke our agreement.

The opposite of an "I" message is a "you" message, and it is usually full of name calling and blame.

A typical "you" message looks like this:

You are a louse and a scum for being so self centered and inconsiderate. You are immature and irresponsible.

Notice in the assertive "I" message, there was a specific feeling and reason which were clearly communicated without blame. In the "you" message, there is no mention of feelings or the behaviors which caused the feelings and there is considerable blame in the name calling and labeling.

Assertiveness is a full expression of yourself. It is based on self-respect, takes into account and honors your feelings, claims your rights as a person, and clearly and directly expresses your needs and desires without diminishing the other person.

"I" messages mean that you claim and own your own feelings. One of my graduate students (I will call her Jamie) wrote very eloquently about this in her journal:

My husband Tom is a very messy person. I've lived with him for almost a year and have known this about him since day one. I know that for me there are other important qualities that are meaningful to me and that his messiness is something that I try to remember is not that important. He is very defensive about it because he has been repri-

manded for it all of his life...by his family and his ex-wife. I knew when I married him he'd always be this way, and I also knew that being as orga- nized as I am it would be a struggle within me.

Whenever I try to get him to do a better job by saying 'you do this, or that,' he becomes defensive. If however, I take full ownership of my problems by saying, 'I've been so frustrated all day because of these little messes everywhere....I'm really hav- ing a hard time not obsessing about the junk left on the living room floor, the dishes left in the den, the crumbs on the kitchen counter, and the trash in the car. I know it's just a small thing and I try to go about my day by ignoring them, but it is really hard for me to do that.' Then I get a positive result...the focus is on me, my frustration, and how we can alleviate some of that frustration and it really does work. He's become so much better about picking up after himself. I truly believe that it is me not him that has the problem when I am frustrated. I have a girlfriend that is a worse slob, and her husband doesn't mind, so there are no problems. Our problem arises because I do mind.

From experience I can say that I get much better results when I take complete responsibility for my feelings and the effects those feelings create for me.

The chart opposite presents contrasting messages compar- ing assertiveness, aggressiveness, and passivity on four feeling dimensions.

Rationalization

One way in which I dissipated some of my angry feelings was to rationalize and give myself messages which challenged the negative experience of my loss. For example:

	ASSERTIVE I message	AGGRESSIVE You message	PASSIVE Anything you want message
FEELINGS			
Betrayed:	*I feel like you broke our agreement and I don't like being treated that way. In fact, I won't be.*	*You scum, etc.*	*It's alright dear, but please don't do it again.*
Hurt:	*I'm also feeling hurt and it's awkward for me to feel this vulnerable.*	*You're a bastard (or bitch). You can't be trusted.*	*I'll be alright in a little while.*
Needy:	*This vulnerability makes me feel too dependent and off-center. I am going to change this.*	*You aren't worth needing.*	*Just stay with me.*
Loving:	*I really want a good love relationship with you.*	*You had better be there and give me love after all I've done for you.*	*I probably don't deserve your love, but I'll take what I get.*
NOTE:	These expressions accept the totality and complexity of the experience and deal with the wholeness of it.	These are all angry responses meant to create blame and distance from the other person.	These all come from a place of low self-esteem.
	Send clear communications and demonstrate self-respect.	Cloud communication with blame and anger.	Cloud communication with self pity and insecurity.
	Are functional, taking appropriate share of responsibility for outcome.	Are dysfunctional; denying responsibility for outcomes and blaming others.	Are dysfunctional; denying responsibility for outcomes and blaming self.

Sweet Lemon: *Well, it's probably all for the best.*

Sour Grapes: *She/he is not the person I want to share my life with anyway.*

Actually in my case, the grapes got kind of sour. I didn't really like the way Winter was treating me as she was trying to disengage from our relationship. I began to admit to myself that the sweetness of the grapes was gone. This was an important waking up for me when I could say to myself that "She has changed, and I don't really like this 'new person.'" Since I was being rejected, it became easier to adopt this attitude.

Rationalizing is an important internal process. It affects your belief system. It's safe to try out new thoughts without committing to them publicly. This was important for me because I didn't want to burn any bridges. I could process my negative thoughts privately. I could put her down in my thoughts with self-talk such as:

Sour Grapes: *She is being cold and distant, and besides, she is not really that pretty.*

Sometimes a little silent name calling or discounting made me feel better without feeling guilty. Creating possible reasons for not loving her were a way of building up my strength for letting go. Deep down I really wanted her to come back and would entertain other rationalizations such as:

Delusion Fantasy: *She will come to her senses and will come back to me and we will return to our prior state of bliss.*

We are taught that rationalization is not a particularly good idea. I don't agree. We need to see that rationalization is a natural human process. It serves us in sorting through and dealing with the pain from the hurt, and helps to dissipate anger and keep it from building up. The trick is to not be trapped into over-rationalizing your feeling experiences because you may be:

> *Band-aiding with the false reassurance of sweet lemon:*
>> *"Oh, I like the way it has turned out."*
>
>> *or*
>
> *Projecting blame with total sour grapes:*
>> *"It's all her fault."*

Self-Affirming Rebuttals

Rebuttals transform negative energy by asserting positive self-affirming counter-statements rather than internalizing the toxic feelings. Affirmations are a way of turning around your angry feelings. Repeating the affirmations below will change the energy behind your anger.

Give yourself the gift of the following affirmations.

> *I am choosing not to be frustrated.*
> *I am choosing not to hate.*
> *I am choosing not to feel inadequate.*
> *There is nothing to be afraid of. I can take care of myself.*

Take a few deep breaths as you say each of these and repeat them several times. Feel yourself getting centered and clear with renewed energy after this affirmation exercise. Use your journal to create additional affirmations for yourself.

Refusing to Give Away Your Power

The person who angers you, by definition, has a measure of control over the way you feel unless you choose to create something different. You can always choose not to put up with betrayal, rejection, or domination by taking yourself out of those relationships. The idea is simple, and straightforward. The actual disengagement from the investment in the relationship is not so easy. The important thing to know is that you do always have a choice. You can start by simply saying the following affirmations to yourself on a regular basis.

- I'm not going to put up with this any longer.
- I'm not giving away my power or my freedom to another person.
- I don't have to stay angry.
- I don't have to get even.
- I can choose to be with people who will treat me well.
- I may not be able to change the other person, but I can change myself, and I can change the situation.
- I have personal power.

AN EXERCISE TO PRACTICE
YOUR ASSERTIVE RESPONSES

Use the following formula to help you simplify and clarify your communication:

I feel... (specific feeling)
when you................................... (specific behavior)
This makes me want to............... (specific reaction)
But what I really want is............ (specific outcome)

Use your journal to continue claiming your feelings and use this formula to help you focus on specifics.

VII. *Last Ditch Search For a Bargaining Chip* 🙠

Bargaining is a little like a drowning man hoping, beyond hope, to grab something that will keep him afloat as he faces the grim alternative of going under. Bargaining comes into play in the final stages of denial, when things are looking very desperate and hope is hard to hold on to. Hope is in fact dying, and about to be snuffed out like the last candle in an already dark room. Bargaining is the last breath of hope.

You still believe there is one last chance, and that maybe if you tried harder, or changed a certain thing about yourself, you might be able to make a deal, and at least try to make a go of the relationship which you don't want to die. You are floundering in the flood of all your sadness, fear and confusion. As the prospect of making it as a couple diminishes there is a depressing anguish as you scan your possibilities and ask yourself "What can I do?"

Willingness to Change

Looking for a way to salvage and restore the love you want so badly is a very natural response in a desperate situation. Most of us would be willing to negotiate a small issue such as toothpaste or other personal habits. Larger issues such as career choices, family proximity, social life priorities, leisure time activities, and willingness to communicate are more difficult to negotiate. You have to ask yourself: "How willing am I to compromise?"

You may be willing to sell even a bit of your soul if it will turn things around. The mind sweeps for schemes to find ways to let you hold on. It is a last-ditch effort. Is there some bargaining chip which will magically restore the love you once knew?

I had a difficult time coming up with what I should or could change. Winter didn't confront me with any major complaints. She said it was just something she needed to do for herself. Since I couldn't figure out what was going wrong, and Winter couldn't really help me understand my part in it, I decided to just be Mr. Wonderful. Surely she couldn't reject Mr. Wonderful.

> I'll be super nice, non-possessive, and strong in my
>   professional competence.
> I'll continue to be interested and supportive but
>   not pushy.
> I'll be open to doing fun things together.

All these intentions were fine, but they didn't make a bit of difference. She already knew that I was a nice guy and so what else was new?

The truth was that I could do nothing to turn things around. Truth had a rude way of pervasive intrusion into my fantasies of making it again with Winter. Truth was like a huge ship cutting through the water, not to be swayed from her course.

People Patterns

Human behavior is for the most part consistent and predictable.[19] We all have ways of being and doing things that are unmistakable and uniquely our own. Some people are, for example:

- always late, others always prompt.

- always neat and orderly, others casual, even sloppy.
- always needing to be right, others don't seem to care about such matters.

These differences sometimes create problems in relationships.

Often we are blind to our own patterns. We can only see them if we are open to hearing about them in non-defensive ways, and if someone is willing to tell us how they perceive us. I believe it is important to have an attitude of openness which says: "You might be right; I will try that on and see if it fits."

Although Winter couldn't really give me any reasons or point to patterns of my behavior which were especially troublesome for her, there were some emerging differences in our lifestyle values around more formal household settings vs. more casual in-the-woods settings. I was willing to negotiate these issues but also knew that they were only the shadow of a larger discontent and shifting priorities going on within Winter.

I felt shut out…as if what was happening with her was private. I also felt that she didn't really understand herself. She just seemed caught up with a compelling movement toward having her separateness.

Two to Tango

Essentially, I couldn't get her to tango anymore. It was frustrating. I had asked her to go for couples counseling with me, and she agreed to go one time. The only thing that came out of this session was her determination to be separate and an unwillingness to continue counseling. Still no issues to confront. I felt a growing sense of hopelessness.

When partners can't talk freely about their feelings, there is a kind of walking-on-eggs dance which is full of tension, pain and avoidance. Walking-on-eggs with your partner is probably the furthest thing from a tango, and is a clear message that this is a relationship that is not healthy. It's just common sense to know that relationships won't work unless both partners want it to work.

Last Vestige of Hope

To say that I had a difficult time letting go of Winter is a laughable understatement, but I also found it difficult to hold on to hope in the face of all that was happening. I looked for any sign of "maybe" for several months. While I was hopeful, I was not totally unrealistic. At some level, I knew that this grieving time was probably a very necessary time for a gentle disengagement. I was refusing to slam the door shut. "See you later," sounded better than "Good-bye."

My last scheme and faint hope was that we would plan a final weekend together in a setting which had been a centerpiece in our courtship. I proposed a March weekend in North Conway. I felt that this romantic setting would be an appropriate and powerful symbol of the good times we shared. We both wanted to end with good memories, good feelings, and good wishes. We agreed that the North Conway weekend would be our last weekend together. It was time to stop the drifting. The weekend would be a closing ceremony as we planned to say our good-byes, immersed in the history of our romance, and acknowledging that it was history.

So it was that I faced our final time together. At some faint level I still hoped that the romantic setting in North Conway would snap her back to her senses. (God—what an optimist!) It was not to be. After almost six years, the first five of which were a very blissful relationship, her sunshine faith was gone. The celebrating was over. It was clear that there would be no going back. I had no influence over the changes which had happened in her.

The Death of Denial

When I realized that there were no bargaining chips and that nothing I could do or say would change things, I knew that I had come to the end of my denial. Hope had evaporated with my last scheme and my final efforts had not begun to phase the tide yet alone turn it back.

This naked truth was my lowest point, and also an important turning point. It was the beginning of waking up and the birth of letting go. Paradoxically, it was a time of profound sadness, and a time of great relief.

VIII. The Low Point is The Turning Point ᔑ

Truth is a predator, it just keeps
coming at you, stalking you...
Always advancing, haunting you, calling out...
Always wanting in.

I had given Winter every opportunity to change her mind. Nothing would work to bring her back to me.

It's over! No more lies to myself. No more hopes
or delusions, no kidding myself.

I realized that I could no longer adorn truth with any embellishments without distorting it somehow. "It's over" means it's over! No more maybes! Without this key admission, there would be no end to my denial; I would remain stuck.

This was the low point I had feared. I had staved off this blunt reality with all the denial I could muster, but truth ran over all my final attempts like a steam roller. Truth had stalked me, was rudely standing there glaring me in the face. There would be no more hiding.

Hope, as my warm blanket of protection, had been stripped away. I felt very exposed and vulnerable.

Where do I go from here?
I guess I start over, but how?

I felt a pervasive sadness, very confused and quite alone.

Truth As Both Painful and Relieving

Although it seems paradoxical, as sad as I felt, I also felt relieved. I had not realized what a heavy burden this armor of denial had been. When I set this armor down for the last time, I felt a new breath of freedom. I had not expected to feel as light and liberated in the face of my sadness and confusion. Hitting bottom did not mean that I bounced back immediately to some new high place which was full of euphoria or even a peaceful sense of well-being; it was just this quiet sense of relief.

Truth, while painful, was a much cleaner platform with a more solid foundation than denial had provided. Denial needed many props of excuses, rationalizations, and delusions which I provided for myself as protection and survival. I realized at some level that I was going to be okay. Even though there was pain, it was not the end of the world. This awakening and acceptance of the truth was the critical turning point in my recovery.

> *I finally let myself see things*
> *the way they really were*
> *and*
> *I didn't like what I saw.*
> *I decided:*
> *I can either do something*
> *about making my life different and better,*
> *or*
> *I can wallow in this 'self pity,' and be a victim,*
> *or*
> *I can slowly start upward toward the light.*

Hitting bottom only leaves you with two options. You can either stay down or start to climb out. It felt good to know that I wasn't going any lower. "It could not get any worse than this," meant to me that in time I would get better. Since I didn't like being down, I started to climb.

While I could get this "I'm-on-my-way-up" message in my head, I still had heartache and a back pain, and terrible waves of sadness washing over me in my alone times.

Headfirst

The thing that I want you to know is that:

When you get this waking up message of "it's over" really clearly in your head, it is the pivotal point—the turning—the absolutely essential bedrock truth-acceptance upon which all your other recovery steps depend.

Start with the truth in your head first; your body and emotions will follow in time. How much time this will take, will vary with you depending on many circumstances. Certainly it will depend on the commitment and level of love you shared with your partner. It will also depend on your support systems of family and friends and your overall psychological makeup.

Don't worry about the time right now, just know that if you get it straight in your head first, that everything else will follow. I'm not sure when I finally felt resolved and integrated with body, mind, and spirit; I just got better within a year or two for the most part as I remember. The fact is, after accepting the truth of finality, I started immediately upward.

It just got easier and easier to be me, an astonishingly new undiscovered me...the me without a partner. This was the first time I had been without a mate in more than twenty years. I was a forty-seven-year-old man, with four sons between the ages of nineteen and ten.

As the weeks passed, my emotions and physical well-being began to accept the messages from my head, and I began to feel more together, more integrated. There was a gradual lifting of my spirits during this time. Since I was no longer deluding myself about my relationship with Winter, there was no new disappointment, just old pain, and this was slowly fading.

Unfolding and Discovering

As a single person, everything would now be different. Everything was new. I had much to discover about myself. A jour-

nal entry some two months after Winter left me reveals that
my faith in myself was a major factor in my recovery process.

> *I'm aware that I'm feeling good about myself these
> past few weeks especially. The wellspring seems to
> be pumping up fresh life.*
>
> *I was just now sitting on a chair and feeling
> (saying to myself): I really love myself, and almost
> feeling embarrassed as if it shouldn't be heard out
> loud. I continued: and of course this really is why I
> can love other people so well.*
>
> *Right now I am able to love Winter very freely,
> not possessively, and I know she feels this and is
> responding herself with a peaceful kind of giving in
> return.*

This did not mean that I was sailing along without pain, it
just meant that I was paying more attention to my possibilities,
and feeling good about myself. It is important to acknowledge
your strength as part of making the turn upward.

I was more and more aware that it was time to get on with
my life, and I was aware that my attitudes had everything to
do with getting through difficult lonely times. It felt great to
turn the corner toward light, and I began to make plans about
what I needed to do in order to take care of myself.

IX. Understanding, Accepting & Forgiving 🐟

*I knew intuitively that if I was going to
move on from the loss, I needed to understand,
I needed to accept, and I needed to forgive.*

Understanding

I needed reasons, even excuses I suppose. I wanted something I could believe in to keep my life in some sort of order. If I could look to external circumstances to find reasons for the break up, it would soften the self-doubt and confusion which I felt. To develop reasons meant I needed information, and Winter could not tell me what was going on with her; perhaps she didn't want to hurt my feelings. Perhaps she was confused herself.

So, I'm scratching my head and saying:

> *What in the hell happened?*
> *How could she have given up on us?*
> *Have I been blind?*

I had to guess at what had happened. At first I thought it was that she had met this wonderful man and that was the reason: He was just more wonderful than I was. While that could well have been the case, I felt like something larger was happening. It felt more as if Winter was having a breakdown rather than a breakthrough. It seemed like some outside force, some alien had come and inhabited her body. It was strange, and I felt helpless. I could hardly contact her, even when I was with her face to face, eye to eye. Incommunicado!

It didn't seem to matter how I behaved, what I felt, or what

I said. The only thing that was clear was that she was gone and I knew it. But why?

I thought back to several months before when I had noticed how she was getting picky about what I thought were little things. For example: my boys occasionally left fingerprint smears on the refrigerator door—or on a white wall somewhere, as they came in from playing outside. Even though these would wipe off easily with a sponge, she seemed overly critical; I thought she was blowing things out of proportion. I began to notice that she seemed to be more tense and stressed. She was coming unglued from the "sunshine faith." There was more tension between us.

In retrospect, I think now that she was experiencing an existential uneasiness, and asking herself: "What in the hell am I doing in this relationship?" "Where is it going?" "Where am I going?"

Since I couldn't figure out what I needed to do to fix things, and Winter couldn't really tell me very clearly, I found myself making assumptions in order to make some sense of it all.

Developing a Story

I needed to have a story. It was important for me to be able to explain to my friends what had happened to Winter and me. I wanted to maintain my sense of self in the face of this rejection. I wanted to save face, and I needed to look beyond blaming myself. "There must be something wrong with me," just didn't compute. When I looked for reasons outside myself and came to conclusions which made sense to me I was comforted and reassured: "It wasn't all my fault!"

Just believing that much was salve for my wounds.

The first assumption I made was that our age difference was the main reason we broke up. No one could argue against the obvious developmental differences.

Some of these differences jumped out clearly:

1. I was forty-seven, she was thirty-two.

2. She was ready for a career change while I was committed to staying put in order to be with my four sons;
3. Did she want to have children? With me?
4. Where would our home be? Would she be stuck on my turf?
5. How would it be to be a stepparent?

All of these are huge issues and were important questions which I believed were unsettling for her.

There were other stress factors pressing on Winter. She had given up her job, her career, and her home to come and live with me when

a) my divorce was not yet final.
b) my sons didn't really validate her as a stepmom. Their loyalties were with their mother, and their hopes were that I would return.
c) Winter felt the community judged her as the "other woman," the one who broke up my marriage and family.

There were of course those in the community who did judge her in a negative way, just as there were those who judged me. For Winter, this was particularly stressful, especially in one case where she was turned down for a job for which she was immensely qualified because she was living with me and we were not married.

It only took one or two experiences of negative judgment to convince her that others might be feeling the same way. Winter had always prided herself on her professional image and to lose the respect of others was a severe blow to her sense of self. She was a strong community person, and her friendships and the respect she earned from others were very important, particularly as these connections enhanced her professional network.

There were money issues now that she was unemployed. She seemed to be more "uptight" about many things in our last year together. Independence became her mission and our togetherness took a back seat.

Stress Changes People

As I began to try to understand what Winter was going through—and what I was going through—I came to see that there were some seven themes which impacted on each of us in varying degrees. The following scale is an attempt to understand more fully the impact and the cumulative effect resulting from these stressful events. The assigned points on this scale are arbitrary; nothing has been validated on any population. The scale was just another way that I used for speculating and trying to understand what happened. Stress will wear a person down as surely as rust will pit the most polished steel surface in a moist environment over time.

Here is how I rated myself, and how I imagined Winter might have experienced these stresses.

STRESS FACTORS CONTRIBUTING TO SEPARATION OR DIVORCE

Event	Possible Points	Rating My Stress Level	My Guess at Winter's Stress Level
1. Change of residence:	10 / 15 / 20	20	35
• *Add 5 to your total for each move in one year*			
• *Add 5 for changing communities*			
• *Add 10 for changing regions of the country*			
2. Change or loss of job:	20 / 30 / 40	—	40
3. Buy or sell a house:	10 / 15 / 20	20	20
4. Financial setback:	20 / 25 / 30	30	30
5. Recent divorce or separation:	20 / 30 / 40	25	20
6. Family or community tensions:	10 / 15 / 20	10	20
7. Isolation from former social network, friends, and family:	10 / 20 / 30	10	30
Total:		115	195

While this Stress Factors Scale[20] may be a piece of the elephant, we can never really ever fully understand the complexities of relationships when they are coming apart. I can imagine and rationalize that people change for all sorts of other reasons including the resurgence of dysfunctional patterns of behavior, chance or created opportunities, and growing self-awareness.

Whether or not any of these reasons were really true, or whether or not I really understood the truth was not the important issue. What was important was that I had reasons that made sense to me, and that creating reasons which I could believe made me feel better, and helped me open up to acceptance and forgiveness.

An Existential Itch

I thought that Winter was having some kind of breakdown, and I also think that breakdowns are often a prelude to breakthroughs. I came to see that since leaving was her idea, she must be on some kind of quest to work through important issues in her life, and to redefine herself. At some level we are all trying to fulfill our potential, as we listen to those inner urgings which call us to express our wholeness, our passion, our creativity, and our sense of wonder.[21] It is an inner drive to discover ourselves and to live our lives fully. This journey for discovery may also be laden with dysfunctional patterns such as the inability to be intimate or to commit, or the distorted notion that the grass is always greener on the other side of the fence. Nonetheless, there is an urge for self-discovery in all of us. The quest is for health, well-being, and peace. For the most part, there is no malice intended toward others as each of us goes about trying to meet our needs, and become the best person we can be. I suspect that these inner drives, be they demons or angels calling, are the real reasons why most people leave relationships. I believe that there is in all of us, a desire to be peaceful and to be happy. There is an ongoing movement toward creating a good life for ourselves, as we are drawn toward what we perceive as our own best options.

I had experienced being the one to leave an earlier relationship with my former wife for reasons of self-fulfillment. This understanding of myself helped me to accept that this must be part of what was happening to Winter when she pulled away from our relationship. It still hurt like hell. I now know more clearly the pain which my former wife Nancy must have experienced when I left. To Nancy's great credit, she was able to love me even as I left. Her example of loving and letting go helped me to create with her a new way for an ongoing sharing of parental joys and responsibilities, and to build a caring, supportive friendship which continues to this day. I care deeply about her and I know she does for me. I have learned that love is the essence of any healthy relationship. Even as partners grow apart it is possible to continue to love and respect each other, and to redefine and restructure your relationship if you have an attitude which is willing. Reasons help you understand, which in turn help you to accept and to forgive.

Accepting

There are two levels of acceptance to reach in the recovery from relationship loss.

1. There is the acceptance that the relationship is over. This is the final admission of what is real and what is a fact, and is reached only after all bargaining has failed and hope is lost. I arrived at this level of acceptance after the North Conway weekend when my last efforts and hopes proved to be futile.

2. There is acceptance of the person who is leaving. This is largely a matter of the heart, but is also tied in strongly with your attitudes and belief system. The undeniable fact was that Winter had changed, and

was in a tremendous upheaval of uncertainty. Believing that Winter was not malicious, but simply trying to work out her own life, made it much easier for me to accept her as a person even as she left me.

Giving Winter the benefit of any doubt, made me feel stronger because I felt like a "good guy." I accepted that she was doing what she needed to do, and that she was doing the best she could with the options she saw. I knew that she was no longer in love with me even though she cared about me. I knew clearly that she was not committed to continuing our relationship. The old cliché: when one person changes, the relationship changes, was blatantly evident and I needed to accept this truth.

No genius mentality is required to see that it would not be good for me to remain in a relationship in which I did not experience the kind of love and commitment that I needed, that I wanted, and that I was capable of giving. Finally I woke up and said to myself: "Who needs to be treated this way? Not me! I'm better off getting out of this relationship. I deserve better." I came to see the truth, and experienced a whole new meaning of the old inscription on the Hall of Letters at the University of Redlands: "The truth will set you free."

Forgiving

You don't have to forgive your former mate if you don't want to, but just know that the person you are really punishing is yourself if you don't forgive. If you don't forgive you don't heal, it is that simple.

What does it mean to not forgive? It means
- you are still angry.
- you still carry the hurt, and are still the victim.

All your thoughts and feelings have an element of choice in them. I am saying you can choose not to experience all the toxic waste of an unforgiving spirit. It only drags you down.

There are two important reasons why people choose not to

forgive, and you should look carefully at these if forgiveness is an issue for you.

1. Not forgiving keeps you feeling angry, hurt, and vulnerable. This will keep you from letting yourself get through your grieving. You may think you are protecting yourself, but in the long run your attitude only blocks your development as a person.

2. Not forgiving allows you to blame the other person, and you hold them responsible for what has happened to you. You may think that others will feel sorry for you or that others will reject your former mate. But this is only a revenge fantasy.

Both of these reasons work against your well-being, happiness, and recovery. Not forgiving is holding onto the past, and you will not go forward with your life if you do not forgive.[22]

Forgiving Does Not Mean Forgetting

Memory is a powerful thing, especially if you have been hurt. If you touch a hot stove, you won't have to be burned too many times before you remember not to touch the hot stove again. Most people who have been burned in romance are a little shy about returning for more. Fortunately the desire for bonding is usually stronger than the fear of being hurt, and we learn to trust again.

Part of learning to trust again is trusting yourself. You come to know yourself as a survivor, and know that you can get through difficult times. Gradually you become willing to risk again.

Some things not to forget:
• You don't like being hurt.
• It wasn't all your fault.
• You learn from experiences.
• There are always choices.

Some other things not to forget:
- You are capable of loving deeply.
- You are basically a loveable person.
- No two people are alike, and the person who rejected you is at a safe distance. You don't need to choose another person like him or her.
- You want to be loved, know how to love, and are improving in your ability to love all the time.
- People change.
- Life is risky.
- You can survive.
- Growth favors flexibility.
- You can change.

Being hurt once does not mean that you will be hurt again, but it could happen, and you will be stronger for the knowing.

Letting Go of Blame

Part of forgiving is just never getting into blaming in the first place. Fault is simply not important.

While your residual anger may keep you from wanting to make life easier for your former mate, when you are able to let go of blame, the wheels of healing are greased in lots of important ways, and this means a more rapid and free recovery for you. When there is no blame, there will be less game playing and less defensiveness which will allow both of you to have more clarity in your communication because it is unencumbered with hidden agendas. Resentment, images of retribution and other ill feelings all remain in the foreground unless there is forgiveness. There can be no freedom without forgiveness because holding on to blame is like holding on to a hot coal which will just burn inside you forever and cause you pain. You don't need this. Your life does not have to be this way because you can choose to forgive.[23]

Before I could get on joyfully with my life, I had to let myself feel my sorrow. I knew that I would not waltz cheerfully and openly into a new relationship. Some things had to be cleared. It was necessary for time to pass. It was necessary for me to go inside and come to know myself more fully. It was also necessary for me to clear my mind of the memories, the images, the symbols, and the places of our high romance.

SUGGESTED EXERCISES

Developing Your Story: Journal Musings
Begin to develop your story by trying to see why your partner is leaving from their point of view. What is going on in their lives? Try to understand and accept those things which happened to your former mate which were beyond your control.

Write these thoughts and observations in your journal. You may wish to list them with the heading: "Possible reasons for the breakup."

Affirmation
Say to yourself:

> *I don't have to forget, but to heal I need to forgive. I can understand, I can accept, and I forgive. As I forgive, I am free. I am in recovery from this relationship loss and I am getting on with my life.*

X. Purging the Ghosts ৎ৯

> *...come fill the cup that clears*
> *today of past regrets and future fears.*
> —Omar Khayyam
> *from the* Rubiyat

Reminders

In the weeks that followed my decision not to pursue Winter with romantic hopes or fantasies, I was more than a little obsessed with wondering what she was doing and thinking. There were constant reminders of her around the house. Picture albums, love letters, and things we had purchased together all called me back to remember the sweetness. There were sweaters she had knit for me, the radio playing our song, beaches, mountains, and restaurants, where we had shared our joy. All of these places and things left behind were trigger points which distracted me from getting on with my life.

Yellow Lights & Pavlov's Dogs

There was no escape from all these reminders since we were still living in the same small town, and her new apartment was located on the route I traveled regularly. The thing that bugged me most about driving by Winter's new place, were these two yellow porch lights. They seemed to always be on, and they would jump out and grab me as I drove by, day or night. I couldn't help but wonder what Winter was doing.

Was she inside?
Was she with someone else?
Was she happy?

Was she missing me?
Did she wish I would stop for a visit?

I found myself getting angry and wanting to go and shoot out those damned lights! I was doing fine when I was not reminded and not remembering, fine when I was not wondering. I felt better when I focused on current activities and people in my life. I wanted to let the past be past. The yellow porch lights just took me down. It struck me one day that I had been conditioned and was no more immune to the laws of stimulus and response than Pavlov's dogs.

What finally helped me to break my conditioning to these powerful reminders was simply to acknowledge to myself that it was happening. In doing this, I was able to stand back and see myself being controlled by two yellow light bulbs. Enlightening! I laughed a little in amusement at how I was caught up in this. Admitting it to myself was all that I needed to break the spell. The lights lost all their power shortly after this awakening and I just never saw them anymore when I drove by. They faded into what they were—two yellow lights.

Reclaiming Nantucket

Nantucket had been a jewel in my romantic excursions with Winter. I knew that if I was ever going to enjoy this island again, I would have to go there to erase old images and memories and build new ones. I knew that letting go of associations to places and things which caused me to live in the past would be important. I didn't want Nantucket to stand out like those two yellow lights. I didn't want to give power to any symbols and ghosts of the past. If I was going to be free in my spirit, I knew that I would need to openly face going to the island alone. I knew that if I did not face my pain and let it out, it would not go away. I took two weeks in May to go to Nantucket to purge the pain and create new experiences and new memories.

I walked the beaches, I rode my bike, and I watched the sun set and the moon rise. I talked to strangers and wished I could meet a beautiful and wonderful woman who would once again make me feel alive. All these activities and fantasies were important outlets for me and helped me break old images by creating new ones. I also did a lot of journal writing in Nantucket. Here is an entry from Siasconsett in the middle of May, just two days into my pilgrimage.

> ...*a gray day.*
> *A cool breeze bridging seasons.*
> *Everywhere blossoms on trees and wildflowers greeting the sun from green earth.*
> *Today I saw a bluebird for the first time. In the last two days, I have seen cardinals, quails, red-winged blackbirds, dove, blue jays, pheasant, geese, ducks, gulls, and several birds I can't identify. I've heard the bobwhite outside my door and I've seen cottontail rabbits.*
> *...thought about Loren (my brother) and wanting to laugh with him.*
> *I walked on the beach and picked up a variety of dead sea life—mostly seaweed with one small crab and a shell from a small scallop. Beautiful the way it all goes together.*
> *When I came to Siasconsett on Sunday, I went for a walk on the shore where the shimmering reflection of the full moon on a quiet sea gave me a most glorious glimpse of being on the earth and reaching outward to the whole universe. A quiet prayer of thankfulness came to me that surely this must be the most beautiful of all planets in this enormous universe.*

It's interesting, in retrospect, for me to read these pieces again and see that while I remember the sadness and grieving, it is clear that Nantucket was more importantly a spiritual uplifting for me. It was an awakening and renewal of my sense of connectedness with life. This moonlit walk on the beach was what Abraham Maslow[24] would call a "peak" experience. I felt jolted by the power of feeling my at-one-ness with the universe. Here is another passage from this same journal entry.

> *Everything is okay. The moon is still there pulling the tides and lighting the sky and shimmering a dance upon the sea. I am alive and well walking the beach, and the planet is healthy and beautiful....All is well.*

Another kind of journal writing I did in Nantucket was to write letters to Winter. Letters which I had no intention of mailing. This outlet for my feelings was direct and clear. It was a voice which had heretofore been stifled. The themes of these letters were aimed at acknowledging all the beautiful joy we had shared, and to say goodbye. Somehow, by honoring our love, I released myself from holding on to the past.

> *It's been painful to return alone to this island paradise without you, and, at the same time, I am loving being here. In a strange way, I am feeling peaceful about my pain. I'm warmed by the fullness of such a love we shared....It feels like a grief-letting that is necessary to remain whole.*

Two days later, I made these journal entries.

> *Thought about Winter and wondered how such a precious love was lost. I felt like we were both in heaven—I feel like I'm still here, but that she has fallen. Quite a puzzle. Perhaps I overestimated her or our relationship. Maybe she just got some blemish—a twist in her personality to knock her off center and out of grace with our love.*

My journal was a private and safe place for me to go inside myself and explore all my feelings. I could give myself permission to express my sadness as well as to allow my hopeful voice to reassure me that I would find a new love. Expressing these often opposing voices gave me a more clear and complete picture of myself.

Nantucket served as a symbol for all the romantic holidays I had taken with Winter, and now I was able to break the 'hold' these places had on me from all these associations. It was a kind of deprogramming which I had intuitively moved toward in my quest for healing. It was a breaking of the bonding between places and past associations and the creation of new experiences.

Images As Triggers

After the Nantucket purging, I began to stand back and see how all these symbols triggered memories and images. I began to see that these trigger points could be useful for opening up my feelings that I had not previously let into my consciousness. My pain had now subsided enough, and I felt that I could let in the reality of what was and what is.

Letters, photo albums, gifts—all these things are opportunities to open up to your grieving, and to complete it. It would be a mistake if you tried to shut these images and symbols out of your mind, to avoid all memory stirrings. Avoidance gives power to that which is avoided. What I learned was that to grieve is not to avoid my pain, but to go into it, purge it, and go beyond.

My last entry from Nantucket was a voice of determination and affirmation.

> *I will find another angel on this heavenly earth,*
> *because I want to love life this way, and because I*
> *know there are others who do also.*

Stepping Back to Observe Ourselves

Men in our culture are not usually known for their introspective qualities. This self-observation is a skill which we need to develop and take time for. It is this taking of time and inward looking wherein we find ourselves and lay claim to our deepest longings and furthest visions.

To enter into this reflective state, we need alone time. A time to quiet ourselves from the distractions and tasks which pull us through the day like a train of connected boxcars chugging down the rails to our day's end. When we are able to stand back and look at our stations and our destinations, we can see the many tracks available to us.

We all have the ability to stand back and see ourselves doing what we are doing. This ability to reflect on our experiences is a powerful source for change because, in standing back, we can evaluate and make choices about how we want to be. We have the ability to see the big picture, to make images for the future, and to daydream about pathways to take us to where we want to go.

It was by observing myself that I began to see my grief more from a distance.

> *Look there is Dwight and he is hurt. Look at his*
> *reactions to his hurt, aren't they interesting? There*
> *he is reacting to those yellow porch lights, really*
> *hoping to still make it with Winter.*

I was beginning to see myself going through this process of grieving and that was an exceptionally helpful awareness. Stepping outside myself, and my situation, allowed me to distance myself from the pain and confusion I was going though. Observing myself, I could see my hurt and my sadness and I began to see better paths to take and choices to make.

XI. The Magic of Optimism: Ten Steps to Making It Work ✍

I had come away from Nantucket feeling renewed and feeling optimistic about life and about myself. The ghosts of my old romantic images had been purged. I had reclaimed the island. I felt a sense of closure in my relationship with Winter. I had begun to let go of the illusions with which I had shackled myself. I felt new freedom and sensed new opportunities. I knew that it was time for me to get on with my life, I felt hopeful and expected good things to happen. It was what I wanted and what I focused on.

A Point of Clarification

This chapter is about being optimistic about your own life with regard to those issues which are within your control, namely your attitudes about circumstances, your choices, and your behaviors.[25] That's a lot!

Being blindly optimistic about circumstances which are beyond your control will certainly create conditions for experiencing disappointments. But for those many conditions which are within your control, you will find that optimism works very well for you. It works because you look closely at your options and your priorities, and you make better choices for yourself.

Optimism Is Learned

The magic of optimism is not that it appears like an object out of nowhere. It is magic because it pays off and feeds on itself, begetting more optimism. An example of this circularity is:

> *You feel good about life because you feel good about yourself, and you feel good about yourself because you feel good about life. It is like a two-cycle reciprocating engine, and choosing positive attitudes is your fuel. For example, believing that life is good and that you have many opportunities, sets up the condition for taking responsibility to create desirable outcomes which result from your positive action. Your view of the world is validated because you look for good everywhere, are open to it, willing to work to make it happen, and find delight in it each time you prove yourself right.*

We learn our life-explanatory style according to what pays the greatest dividends. When you were growing up, if you were rewarded with lots of admiration and praise, and received status from your family and your friends when you behaved in a cynical or skeptical manner, your behavior and your attitudes were shaped by those reinforcing payoffs. Likewise if you were given lots of admiration, praise, and status when you were positive and hopeful, these optimistic behaviors and attitudes would be your outlook on life because of the good feelings generated, which were reinforced by acknowledgement.

Belief Systems Are Self-Generating

Here is how it works. It is like the four seasons, where each season prepares the ground and conditions for the next. There is a built-in interdependency to the cycle.

OPTIMISTIC MODEL

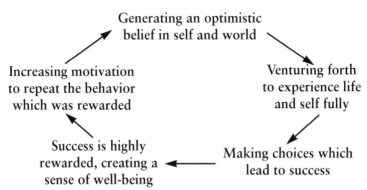

I was fortunate to discover rather early in life that optimism worked for me. In my growing up years, there were significant people who supported me in this belief. I received recognition, acceptance, and validation for my optimistic ways. I learned that if I was positive in my expectations, I could get through difficult times. Achieving some measure of success in things that were important to me gave me faith in myself. Faith in yourself is another way of saying there is self-confidence, and it is from this base that people are willing to venture forth to new experiences and growth. The danger with this kind of positivism is in being overly hopeful in difficult times. This characteristic of mine kept me a little longer in denial than I need to be.

PESSIMISTIC MODEL

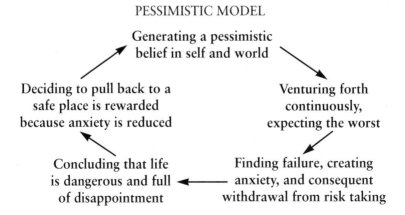

If your family and friendship support network has reinforced your skepticism or negativism, you will have to work
harder to build faith and confidence in yourself and in your
world. If you find yourself with a lot of negative self-talk, you
will need to counter your negativity with affirmations in order
to change your belief system. For example:

Negative Voice:	*I was betrayed and I'm not going to trust being intimate again.*
Countering Optimistic Voice:	*My hurt is from a specific experience, and it does not mean that intimacy should be avoided.*
Affirmation:	*I will find another person to love with whom I can build a life.*

If you have been discouraged rather than encouraged,
how do you regain faith and build confidence? How do you
rebuild that hope inside which has been crushed and buried,
covered over with doubt and cynicism? Most adults have
experienced some disappointments and failures along the
way. We are told that these are good lessons for dealing with
the realities of the world. This is called the School of Hard
Knocks.

To be optimistic and idealistic is often considered to be
naive by adults who are jaded by their own disappointments.
These are people who have long since given up their own
sense of hope, and don't like to see it in others. Many men in
particular have surrounded themselves with armor to protect
themselves from anyone who would put them down for their
optimism and idealism. I have tasted the disdain of those
who thought I was too much of a Pollyanna. I have also
learned that it is important to consider the source of such
criticism, and to realize that those who judge me are really
saying more about themselves than they are about me. If I
empower them by believing them, I am at anchor in their harbor of limitations.

Ten Things You Can Do

The following ten steps will be a guide for you to build your optimism and will help you to restore your faith and confidence in yourself and in your world of experience.

1. Examine Your Belief System

I am asking you to examine your attitudes, values, opinions, priorities and all the behaviors which go into making up who you are as a person.

> *Are they working for you?*
> *Do they keep you stuck?*
> *Are you open to grow?*
> *to tap into your potential?*

Tunnel vision, or rigid and absolute thinking, will close out your options and increase your chances for psycho-sclerosis or hardening of the categories.

Change will require you to entertain new ideas and divergent thinking. It will require you to be experimental as you weigh and try out your options. It will require you to look within. Change is never easy. Patterns of behavior are difficult to repattern, but change is possible if you are willing to believe it and willing to try it.

The following table, Polarized Viewpoints, provides you with an opportunity to see yourself on a variety of dimensions.

We all fall somewhere between the poles of these perspectives of our world as we experience it. Where you are on these optimism vs. pessimism issues will affect your attitudes about recovery and well-being. A pessimistic person will expect the outcome to be negative in order to fulfill his or her prediction that things will turn out badly. The optimist, on the other hand, does not expect any outcome that isn't to his or her advantage.

You wouldn't be reading this book and trying to recover from your loss if you had not already decided that you want to take advantage of your optimism and faith in yourself, even

POLARIZED VIEWPOINTS

PESSIMISTIC . . . . OPTIMISTIC

scarcity . . . . abundance

isolation . . . . intimacy

fear . . . . hope

ill tempered. . . . . warm sense of humor

no goals . . . . goal oriented

illness. . . . . wellness

skepticism . . . . faith

Take a minute now to place an **X** where you see yourself at this time, and place an I where you would like to see yourself as an Ideal you.

Ask yourself: What do I believe about getting over this loss? There are lots of options. For example:

I'll never get   **I will recover and grow**
over this loss . . . . **from this experience.**

Our attitudes about the outcomes in our lives depend largely on how we see ourselves. Here are some other contrasts on a continuum, and you can again place an **X** where you see yourself at this time, and an I for your ideal self.

I am weak. . . . . I am strong.

I am a victim. . . . . I am a survivor.

                                              I am attractive and
I am not very attractive . . . . . . **can become more so.**

                                              I am physically fit and
I am not physically fit . . . .**can become more so.**

if that hope is just a glimmer at this point. Admit that you do hope that your life will work out for you very well indeed. Admitting it will help make it happen.

2. Take Responsibility to Choose
I had to ask myself: "What do I really want? Am I willing to commit myself to going after it?"

I knew that I wanted to be in a committed, intimate, and spiritually bonded relationship. I knew that I would look for that and be open to it. I also knew that while luck might enter in, a large part of what I get in my life experience is what I plan and take responsibility for creating.

Making clear these judgments of what I really wanted put them in focus for me. The following is a journal entry four months after Winter left.

> *When I wake up in the morning, I have choices. Ultimately I am free to choose to be happy or to choose to be sad. Happiness feels better! My goal is happiness, which is to get what I want, or can imagine I want, without interfering with the rights of others.*

Looking back on this journal entry, I see how holding that positive sense of freedom of choice helped me to get on with my life. On the morning of each day, I have considerable influence on how that day will go for me by the very way I choose to view my circumstances and my options. I must be willing to own and claim those value judgments that define life the way I would like it to be for me.

3. Believe What You Want is Possible
To follow the recovery path in the remaining chapters may require you to change your belief system. Before you can know what you really want, you must examine what you believe is possible.

You need to believe that you are going to be well and happy; that you will be fine. You know it is really what you want. Own this feeling and honor the belief that it is possible.

There may be unexplored negative feelings you have about your self-worth. If there is a destructive voice within you which says: "You don't deserve to be happy in a love relationship," you need to examine where this voice is coming from. Ultimately you will have to counter that negative message with a positive rebuttal: "Yes, I can have happiness in a love relationship and I deserve it."

Our belief systems are shaped by our family and cultural architects who draw our boundaries. They become that which make us feel safe and know who we are. When we challenge our beliefs, we threaten the very fundamental view we hold of ourselves: where we stand, how we are known, and how we define ourselves in the world. Challenging your long-held belief systems will not be easy.

- There are patterns which we establish and hold on to. We have ways of behaving which are secure, comfortable, and easy to fall into.
- We have slogans, or sayings we tell ourselves in order to maintain our beliefs and our identity.
- We don't want to be seen as wishy-washy and inconsistent.
- There is an internal sense which says we should be true to ourselves and all the beliefs we hold. Anything less than fidelity to ourselves is seen as a very fundamental betrayal.

At the same time, there is an intuitive voice in you which says: "The old ways are not working." A new emerging voice is saying: "I need to change some things about myself. I can alter my attitudes and my behavior if I choose to." There is a forceful voice in you which says: "I can grow not just survive." These voices are the affirmations you need to construct your optimism. You will need to be disciplined in practicing these affirmations because any protective armor you carry will fend off the threat of change. For men, this armor may be quite thick for defending against feelings.

EXERCISE

In your journal, write down several positive things which you would like to achieve. Underscore the affirmation which highlights your responsibility.

For example: "I want to be well and happy, and to share my life with an intimate partner. *I will work to achieve this.*"

For now, focus on two or three things which will help you achieve your goal, and write them out. Repeat these affirmations several times daily for a week or until you begin to see and feel a shift toward really believing these affirmations, and find yourself behaving in ways to make them happen.

4. Get an Image of What You Want

We all have the ability to visualize ourselves in time and space. For example, you can easily get a picture of yourself having breakfast this morning. You can also look ahead and see yourself in an activity which will roll around for you next summer.

These images, which sometimes flow as daydreams, are the stuff from which our psychic energy goes forward. We begin to get pictures of what we would like. Here is another journal entry.

> *I must first imagine that much is possible. As I get a picture of what I want, I begin to see the steps of what it will take to get me there.*

Victor Frankl in his book, *Man's Search for Meaning*,[26] tells of the ordeal of a young woman in a German concentration camp. He tells us of how she gained strength by focusing on a tree which she could see from a window in her cell. Although the tree was barren in the winter season, she knew that there would be green leaves and abundant growth in the springtime. Seeing herself as alive, even with imposed dormancy, she talked with the tree and identified her own spiritual strength. The lesson is that: it is important for you to visualize your recovery as you blossom from your own barren winter.

As we daydream, we get ideas and gather images; we begin to form goals and build a coherent and believable picture of the way we want our lives to be.

The images we hold will tend to be fulfilled unconsciously because we will intuitively behave in ways to act out what we see on our unconscious screen. If we see blaming and anger, we will project these onto all our experiences, and tend to dwell in them. If we project light, love, power, and joy, then this is what we will plant and what we will reap. My concern is that those who won't let themselves imagine or believe there can be a better way, probably won't see opportunity even when opportunity presents itself.

EXERCISE

Take time to be alone and to let yourself daydream and imagine your full and happy recovery. Do something good for yourself each day that will help you reach these goals you envision.

5. Chase Out Fear and Doubt

To adopt a pessimistic view of your world is to limit the range of your possibilities. If you are full of skepticism, you are essentially telling yourself: "It will never work! Stop exploring and trying. Don't dream of anything better."

Our culture gives us cliches to let ourselves off the hook. This means we don't have to try. We can choose to remain helpless, and to suffer the disappointment which we expect. For example we learn to say: "I'm doing the best I can," and "Nothing can be done," or "What will be, will be" as we learned in the old song *Que Sera, Sera.* Consider the following examples of how you may put yourself down, and write in your journal such self put-downs which may be uniquely yours.

SOME WAYS WE PROGRAM NEGATIVITY
(Mark where you see yourself on the continuum)

	MOSTLY TRUE	SOMETIMES TRUE	NOT TRUE
I am no good. (I'll spoil any relationship.)	. . . .		
I am not worthy. (Everyone else is better and deserves more.)	. . . .		
I am not competent. (Don't look to me for leadership—I'll take what comes.)	. . . .		
I can't do it. (Why try?)	. . . .		
I am not attractive. (And I can prove it by presenting myself in the most unattractive way.)	. . . .		
I am not smart. (I really feel stupid.)	. . . .		
I am different than others. (I'm a little weird; nobody would like me.)	. . . .		
I can't have what I want. (I don't deserve much.)	. . . .		
I am nasty. (This helps me keep distance from others so I can be safe.)	. . . .		
I deserve to be miserable (I should punish myself.)	. . . .		

Noticing these negative or cynical attitudes in yourself will help you begin to screen out that which is self-defeating. If we predict failure, we build a prophesy that is self-fulfilled. Here are some examples, of how you can chase out negative self talk.

Negative Self-Talk	Positive Self-Talk
I can't do it.	*I think I can do it.*
It will never work.	*Something will work out.*
It is hopeless.	*I'll find a way.*
It is no use.	*If I work, I can do it.*

When we give value to a particular belief, we are in effect programming our minds, just as surely as we can program computers. If I tell my brain computer that "I am okay," then my behavior (print out) will be okay. This is the same reason that placebos work. We believe they will work, and our body cooperates with our belief. Belief is a powerful program we write for ourselves, and sometimes these beliefs are distorted. David Burns[27] details how it is that we create distortions in our thinking. A synopsis of his ideas follows:

COGNITIVE DISTORTIONS

1. **All-Or-Nothing Thinking.** You see things in black-and-white categories. If your performance falls short of perfect, you see yourself as a total failure.
2. **Overgeneralization.** You see a single negative event as a never-ending pattern of defeat.
3. **Mental Filter.** You pick out a single negative detail and dwell on it exclusively so that your vision of all reality becomes darkened, like the drop of ink that discolors the entire beaker of water.
4. **Disqualifying the Positive.** You reject positive experiences by insisting they "don't count" for some reason or other. In this way you can maintain a negative belief and look for confirmation in your everyday experiences. You also discount compliments.
5. **Jumping to Conclusions.** You make a negative interpretation even though there are no definite facts that convincingly support your conclusion.
   a. **Mind Reading.** You arbitrarily conclude that someone is reacting negatively to you, and you don't bother to check this out.
   b. **The Fortune Teller Error.** You anticipate that things will turn out badly, and you feel convinced that your prediction is an already established fact.
6. **Magnification: Catastrophic or Minimization.** You exaggerate the importance of things (such as your goof-up or

someone else's achievement), or you inappropriately shrink things until they appear tiny (your own desirable qualities of the other fellow's imperfections). This is also called the "binocular trick."

7. **Emotional Reasoning.** You assume that your negative emotions necessarily reflect the way things really are: "I feel it, therefore it must be true."

8. **Should Statements.** You try to motivate yourself with shoulds and should–nots as if you had to be whipped and punished before you could be expected to do anything. "Musts" and "oughts" are also offenders. The emotional consequence is guilt. When you direct "should" statements at others, you feel anger, frustration, and resentment.

9. **Labeling and Mislabeling.** This is an extreme form of over-generalization. Instead of describing your error, you attach a negative label to yourself: "I'm a loser." When someone else's behavior rubs you the wrong way, you attach a negative label to him: "He's a Goddamn louse." Mislabelling involves describing an event with language that is highly colored and emotionally loaded.

10. **Personalization.** You see yourself as the cause of some negative external event which in fact you were not primarily responsible for.

Ultimately your negative voices will feed any depressing thoughts you may have. The positive voices, on the other hand, will instill hope and help you to create images which focus on what you can do to take responsibility for making happen what you really want to happen.

6. Create Rebuttals

All put-downs are destructive and full of distortion. If you are saying negative things to yourself, it will be necessary for you to work diligently to create rebuttals. It will be important to write out a new script expressing just the opposite of any negative programming. For example: "I am good! I am worthy!

Competent! and so on." Even if you don't yet believe it, write it out and put your name on it.

I, _____, am a good person.
(place your name here)

The danger is: if we do not offer rebuttals to pull us away from our negative self-statements, we will remain locked into our depression and low self-esteem.

7. Expect Positive Outcomes

It is a well known truth that we tend to get what we expect.[28] We filter all our experiences through our belief system. We hold onto that which supports our beliefs. If I believe the world is not abundant, then I will not expect to find much. If I expect the worst in life, I will likely find it because I will be looking for it at every crossing and open to it to prove myself right (as if being right was more important than truth or possibility). For example, if you believe that people can't be trusted, this is what you will find to prove yourself right.

We like to be right.

- It helps us save face.
- It makes life more predictable if we can find or create evidence that our view of the world is accurate.
- It helps us feel strong because we can point out our convictions that have been validated.
- We might even be admired and respected.

Expectations play a huge part in the direction our lives take. People tend to perform and behave very much as they believe they are capable of doing. If we believe that we are not very capable, or entitled, it is likely that this is how we will behave. I discovered the opposite is also true. If I believe that the best outcomes will occur, I will likely find them because I will be looking for them and open to them, and try to create them.

If we expect good things as we face new experiences, we will put out positive energy which attracts other people, and we will increase our chances for getting what we want. This is not to say that every success factor is within our total control, (there are clearly outside circumstances), but in long-range matters of our own choosing, in which we define how we would like to be, our expectations play a significant part.

8. Being Open and Flexible

Being open and flexible means avoiding black-and-white, right-and-wrong thinking. Words like always and never are avoided because they have rigidity, particularly if they are uttered publicly. Here are examples of moving toward more flexible self-talk. If you are feeling betrayed, you might say:

Rigid:	*I don't trust this person, and I never will trust anyone again.* Notice the absolute "never" and the generalization "anyone."
More Flexible:	*I don't trust this person now, and perhaps I will never trust him or her again.* Notice that this statement is time specific—"now," suggesting I might feel differently later. "Perhaps," leaves things in the maybe. This statement is specific to "him" or "her," and not generalized. There are no fixed or negative predictions.
Options Are Open:	*I have been hurt by this person, and I am choosing, for now, not to trust him or her.* Notice the specific feeling—"hurt," the decision—"I choose," and the specific person—"him" or "her." In this latter case, the feeling behind the mistrust is recognized.

One of the reasons men, in particular, often take dogmatic, absolute positions, is that we have been conditioned to take a tough stand. We have learned that if we are flexible, we will be seen as wishy-washy, having no convictions. Men feel that such a judgment will lower their status with their peers, their power, and in an evolutionary sense, their survival. Our consciousness is shifting, and our culture is moving away from this bravado which has been carried over from even pre-historic times. The truth is, our friends won't condemn us for being open and flexible. We are learning that to show our vulnerability is a strength because it is honest and congruent with what is happening in our lives.

9. Keeping the Faith: Affirming Your Intentions

Human intention may be the most powerful force in the world.

Faith captures our most deeply-held human thoughts, feelings, and convictions. It encompasses hope and is founded in the belief that a) the world is good and can be trusted, and b) I am capable of creating and deserve having that which I want and expect to be forthcoming. Holding these beliefs is an inner expression of my faith.

As you change your belief system toward being more optimistic, you may feel at times that your confidence is a thin mask and that your faith could be shaken. In these moments, affirming your intentions will help you project confidence and strengthen your belief in yourself. Others will pick up on the optimism you project, and will see your good fortune as no surprise. The opposite is also true, if you project doubt, others will believe you don't really feel that you deserve positive things to happen.

An Affirmation

I am entitled to that which I choose which is in my best interest.

As you affirm this, you will come to believe that you deserve that which you choose. I think most of us have a fear of staying stuck, and not moving through to a satisfactory outcome. This fear motivates us to act in our own survival interests. For example: If I am afraid that I will never love again, I must do something to prove to myself that I am capable of loving again. Love is our most basic survival instinct, and the motivation to seek love is very strong. Most people who are afraid to love again, deep-down hope that they will love again. It is this hope to which faith is attached.

Fear As Negative Faith

Fear may be an unconscious way in which we sabotage ourselves. If I am afraid to become intimate, this fear will be communicated to my partner as a lack of faith in myself and in her. I may be signaling this fear and self-doubt as a way of preventing me from loving again in order to protect myself. The same is true if I am afraid that my partner might leave me. I would be, to some extent, predicting it and expecting it. If I project fear, insecurity, and uncertainty about being in a relationship, I present myself as being unworthy of equal respect and mutuality in a relationship.

Cast Out Fear!

10. Taking Responsibility for Making Happen
What You Want to Happen

Loss can be a powerful and accelerated time for learning and growth. There is a void created where there was once a rich experience. This gradual emptying out and fading of memories connected to the past, creates the conditions for rebirth.

We come to realize that if we are to survive and to carry on, we must do something. We must act! Our personal crisis requires us to somehow create a new experience.

My pilgrimage to Nantucket gave me a belief that I could

create this newness. I knew that I would need to take responsibility for making happen what I wanted to have happen.

Scanning Options

> *There are so many things to see, activities and avenues to pursue, people to meet that I wonder how I will find the time to do all that I would dream of doing.*
>
> *I can go for a walk on the beach or in the woods; go to church; read a book; call a friend; go to a movie, museum, or concert; pet my dog; water my plants; listen to music, and on and on…*

In the above journal entry, I focused on life's possibilities to avoid feeling victimized. I realize that I, like others, am a complex person with edges of growth in being a better parent, in being a more effective professor and counselor, artist and musician, builder and whatever. All of these dimensions challenge me. Lots to do.

Claim This Affirmation…

> *There are unlimited possibilities of things to do and places to go. I am aware that I make choices about prioritizing and providing balance in my life. I realize that the decisions I make and the activities I choose are totally my responsibility.*

Getting Ready for the Next Step

It is to your advantage to assume an attitude of optimism about recovering from your loss. Since our brain is a lot like a computer, we program ourselves with optimism or pessimism. The printout we get in life, depends on the beliefs, attitudes, intentions, and decisions we put into our computer-like brain. The quality of our output is equal to the quality of our input.

I hope you can see that your attitude toward life has a lot to do with what you get out of life. If you can get your mind set on an optimistic track, all the rest will be taken care of. With optimism, there is a much greater chance that you can experience more of yourself, more awe, more wonder, more reverence, and more gratitude in your life.

Another Affirmation to Claim

I believe it is a plentiful world for meeting my needs and wants, I will find ways to nurture myself. I am eager to be in the world, to explore and find satisfaction in each encounter and experience in my life.

As I open to my world of possibilities, I begin to let myself imagine my options. I am able to visualize choosing and finding my own best path.

I expect good things for myself as I prepare to make a plan to get where I want to be.

Suggested Exercises
- Say to yourself the following affirmations:
  - I am a survivor.
  - I can trust my inner wisdom and strength.
  - I can tap into these powers within.
  - I will let myself be hopeful and optimistic, knowing that this will bring good things to me.
  - I can choose to become what I want to become.
  - I believe these things to be true.
- Make a list of any negative beliefs you hold about yourself.
- Be willing to suspend these beliefs for one week, and keep extending it.

- Catch yourself in self-discounting and refuse to put yourself down.
- Be open to listening to optimistic viewpoints which oppose your negative self-talk and make a list of rebuttals to counter your discounting.
- Look for negative self-talk and catch yourself doing it and immediately say: "Stop it...these things are not true." Then counter with a positive statement that affirms you as a person. For example:
  – I am a good person.
  – I am worthy and I deserve love.
  – I am confident and intelligent and I can do many things.
  – I am unique and have many wonderful characteristics.
  – I choose to be happy and to celebrate life.
- Picture yourself being successful in getting what you want that is good for you.

XII. Roadmap for Healing ✍

Who will not choose health and well being?
Who will not choose fullness and joy in life?

When I came through my denial, I muddled around for a while trying to understand, accept, and forgive. But at the same time, I was ready to get involved with trying to build the kind of future I wanted. Mostly I was ready to get involved with a woman with whom I could make a future.

Follow Your Intuition

It's not that I mapped out every step of my recovery, but at this stage of acceptance of my loss, I knew that I had to get on with my life, and not leave things to happenstance or to go on drifting. Finding direction was more a matter of listening to my heart and to my intuition.

Since we are programmed for survival, what we need to do is to cooperate with ourselves in trusting our inner wisdom to guide us to our healthiest and strongest way of being. This means: thinking, feeling, remembering, dreaming, and imagining all our best options and courses of action. This computer-like programmed inner wisdom of ours has the ability to scan our options, prioritize our values, envision our outcomes, and to evaluate and choose pathways to get us where we want to be. It is with this inner balance that we make our best decisions. We must look within and dare to ask ourselves what it is that we really want.

We will each ultimately go along our own path, at our own pace, as we move through our grieving and on to full recovery. What is clear is that choosing plays a very large part in creating what we want that path to be. There is something in each of us which wants to choose our own best path. This idea is captured in the song *I Did It My Way* which was made popular by Frank Sinatra some years back. I am saying that you should trust your own intuition and the incredible survival instincts which are behaviorally and genetically programmed for your survival. Our survival favors perception, imagination, and a sharp memory as ways of learning and knowing. With all this evolved intelligence, we are able to make judgments about what we do to move ourselves toward attaining our highest potential. Intuition is the summary input of all you know from all your experience. This is the knowledge base provided for your best judgment in decisions. You will use it because you are programmed for survival.

Whole Brain Choosing

We have these two hemispheres of our brain which give balance to our awareness. One side of our brain is task oriented, sequential, organized, and deals with all which is considered to be logical and rational. The other side is capable of awe and wonder, joy and bliss. This is our poetic, musical, and spiritual side. The list below gives examples of right and left brain messages which play in the background and serve to form the foundation of our decision making and consequent actions.

Typical Left Brain Messages:	Typical Right Brain Messages:
• make a plan, Dwight	• find your balance
• start today	• relax, breath deeply
• set up your best conditions	• get centered
• build for success	• listen to some music
• do this next	• go for a walk
• analyze and evaluate	• you need a rest

Women typically are more expressive of right brain activity. The cliché "woman's intuition" suggests that women have an inner sense about matters which transcends logic and analysis. Men also have this intuitive wisdom, it just has not been as developed or valued. In most adult male circles, approval is still based on tangible "performance based" criteria. However, there is a slight shift occurring now as we see such type A personalities frequently becoming the objects of pity because of their narrowness rather than being held in esteem for their material collections.

These right and left brain messages interact, and we try to find balance as we face our choices for change. The mind is our choice maker. Intuition is our key player as we mediate our perceptions, our beliefs, our decisions, and our actions. This inner wisdom serves as observer, monitor, and designer of all that we will become. We are an integrated system as mind, body, and spirit.

All our choices are ultimately based on our judgment of "what is in my interest?"

Making Value Judgments

We make value judgments and decisions for everything we do, even if it is a decision not to decide or a decision to do nothing. The fact is that most of us do something, even if it is very passive, and this something always involves some choice. Here is an activity to help you examine your value judgments and choices.

TWENTY THINGS I LOVE TO DO

List below the first twenty things that come to your mind. Don't think twice, just write them down as quickly as you can.

1. _____

2. _____

3. _____

4. _____

5. _____

6. _____

7. _____

8. _____

9. _____

10. _____

11. _____

12. _____

13. _____

14. _____

15. _____

16. _____

17. _____

18. _____

19. _____

20. _____

Now read over your list and place an

(**A**) for those activities you do alone.

(**I**) for those that involve intimacy.

(**R**) for those that require risk.

(**6**) for any that you have done in the past six months.

If you are neglecting to do the things you say you love to do, what does this say about your priorities or your stuckness and patterns? Perhaps you need to rethink your list and drop those things which don't belong anymore. Or you may want to balance your intimacy, alone time, and risk factors, and create new activities. Reflect on these things and make journal entries as a way of exploring new directions.

For me, what helped things work was:

1. I could see that I had options.
2. I could choose from among these options.
3. I could take action toward achieving my chosen goals.

Choosing to Change

Deciding is a damned hard thing to do.
It means being willing to take risks.

Choosing is standing up to the drifting that has been going on and deciding on a direction you believe to be best for you. We don't always see that to change requires choosing to change. We resist change because it is the unknown that feels unsafe. Most of us like to have consistency in our relationships with people that are important to us. We develop predictable characteristics and patterns in our ways of being. Staying stuck in your status quo may feel safer than risking change, but it is a little like the ostrich whose head is buried in the sand. The greater risk is to hide out and not change.

As we examine our choices and draw upon our intuitive knowing, we find our own best healing path. Movement toward finding this path will not occur unless we see that we have choices and that choices have to be made. In some ways, it may seem easier to just do nothing. You must resist staying stuck. The key to breaking out of this paralysis is to envision your options.

Breaking Free of Worn-Out Patterns

If we are to find new pathways out of our numbness and our dilemmas, we will need to examine our habitual patterns which keep us stuck. These habitual patterns create the boundaries

which define us and keep us predictable and known to ourselves and to others. If the patterns get entrenched and rigid, we
are in danger of stagnation. We may feel safe, but we are on a
treadmill to nowhere if we don't adapt and change.

Practice

Review the checklist below, and note any items which may
apply to you. Use your journal to add to the list, and to examine your feelings and thoughts. In your journal musings, let
yourself dare to imagine changing. Look for worn-out patterns of your attitudes and behavior which no longer serve
you well. For example:

- I am too lazy.
- I have bad habits.
- I can't do it.
- It costs too much.
- I tried it before.
- I'm out of shape.
- I never was any good at that.
- others...

Once you have identified what patterns you want to
change, you must go about breaking these patterns. Here is a
sample formula which is not simple to carry out.

BREAKING PATTERNS

Step One	•Identify your patterns.
Step Two	•Decide to change.
Step Three	•Make a plan.
Step Four	•Commit to your plan.
Step Five	•Discipline yourself and stay the course you set.

AN EXERCISE

Take a few deep breaths, and relax as you exhale, letting go of
your tension. Picture yourself doing very well without the

burden of your worn-out patterns. Give yourself permission to be your best self.

Say to yourself:

> I, _____, accept the wisdom of my
>   *(your name here)*
> inner conscious mind (intuition) in directing me to
> my highest good.

Daydreaming of Possibilities

Daydreaming is another way we access our "right" brain and we can learn to give ourselves over to such reverie by getting off the task treadmill. I needed to let myself daydream and get a vision of what the bright side of the coin looked like, and how I could get myself there. What did I really want? Did I really believe it was possible? One of the things which helps me keep moving, is to let in images of what could be, that is, to daydream about possibilities. When achievement and other purposeful activities get too stressful, we escape into reverie and relax into what we can imagine. Daydreaming breaks us free from our busy business. We have the ability to picture ourselves acting out these images of what we truly want for ourselves, and in this way, we move from the dream image to the real world of action and immediacy. The idea is not to get stuck in the dream so much that you are not able to move into taking on the responsibility to choose to act and then to act!

We all need "alone" time which is so important in providing an opportunity for reflection and the integration of our experiences. This reflection stimulates creativity in our continuing development. Alone time is a spiritual bank account, upon which we draw each day for envisioning our possibilities.

I needed to be in the world of people to meet my needs for intimacy and belonging. For me, people are a natural healing force, and I knew that by setting up such encounters, I would be creating the possibility for new relationships and healing experiences. I sent out signals that I was interested and available.

Dating

It had been six or seven months since Winter had moved out and we had been in this separation dance which had gone on long enough. Now it was time to date other people.

> But who?
> Where would I find a partner?

These were unsettling questions, and I was eager to start my search to answer them. Choosing to date was a turn towards the unknown. I felt full of possibilities as well as full of confusion. Even with doubts and uncertainties, it felt good to be in the next phase of my journey to recovery.

My first date was with Paula. This was clearly a rebound situation for me. I felt awkward in trying to be intimate with her. I was not as free and ready to be with her as I thought I would be. My uncertainty and confusion kept me from really being fully present with Paula. I had too recently turned the corner on the upward climb from my lowest point.

Rebuilding Your Social Network

As your inner world begins to settle down and balance, you must nourish your growing self from every available source. Part of doing well for yourself is to reach out, to build new bridges with people. Relationships provide opportunities for you to discover and express yourself as you continue your development. For many people, social interaction may feel risky because of previous disappointments and hurt feelings. But to not take the risk toward reaching out to others, is to run the greater risk of becoming socially isolated. You may feel safe in your isolation, but you will not develop yourself fully if you fail to connect with others in significant and intimate ways.

- We all need to belong.
- We all need a sense of community.
- We all need to be:
  - acknowledged
  - welcomed
  - accepted
  - cared about
  - listened to
  - respected
  - loved

We are entitled to being treated this way by the very fact that we are members of the human family. Love is our birthright, we deserve it, and we must claim it.

Family, and a community of friends who care about us, provide nurturing sources of strength and stability. It is with people that we find the fullest expression of ourselves:

- our sense of family
- our sense of humor
- our freedom of expression
- our sexuality
- our meaningful work

Everything interconnects. All these pieces make up the richness of our lives. We have so many facets to discover and develop.

FIVE IDEAS FOR DEVELOPING
YOUR SOCIAL NETWORK

1. Stop being in relationships which are damaging or are not supportive.
2. Reflect on the people in your life with whom you would like to improve your relationship. In your journal, list one thing you could do to make these improvements happen.
3. Visualize what you need to do to create healthy relationships with caring friends.

4. Imagine the social contexts in which you will most likely find an intimate partner and potential soul mate.
5. Create positive images of yourself getting on with rebuilding your life. The images you hold will tend to be fulfilled unconsciously because you intuitively will behave in ways to play out what your unconscious screen is projecting. If you project light, love, power, and joy, then this is what you will plant and what you will reap.

Your roadway for recovery will be found within. To summarize the chapter, you will see that to create that map will require you to:

- follow your intuition.
- make value judgments.
- choose to change.
- break free of worn-out patterns.
- visualize your possibilities.
- rebuild your connections to healthy relationships.

XIII. Sources of Strength ❧

While my grieving was very much an inner matter, this inner struggle was made easier by the nurturing I received from my outer world. I intuitively knew, even in the earliest stages of my grieving, that I needed to keep in contact, and in some cases, renew contact with close friends. I wanted to spend time with people and share good times as a break from the pain of my aloneness. I needed to reach out and, in a sense, get outside my self-absorption. I wanted more texture and vitality than I could find in reflection, I needed to do something, and preferably not alone. Connecting socially for friendship time and recreation got me outside myself, and gave me balance. It also created the opportunity for me to let others express their caring, an experience that is not always easy.

Socializing is only one avenue we may have to renew ourselves, people pull their strength from many sources:

God
Sense of humor
Beauty
Reverence
Family; Friends
Intimacy; Challenge
All of the Above

I gain strength from all of these. All of our sources of

strength are interconnected and part of our whole tapestry as a person. We become weavers in this fabric of our own lives as we take responsibility to bring each strand into our experience. To access our inner strengths, we often need connections to outer experience. For example, I may need to be with a friend to enliven a humorous event and share the wonder of laughter; I may need to be alone by a lake in the woods to know a particular peace, beauty and reverence.

In this chapter, I want to share with you the ways in which my men friends particularly have been, and continue to be, of great support to me. It is my hope that you will be encouraged to reach out, to initiate contact with friends, and develop your social network as part of your recovery.

Nurturing the Spirit: A Tribute to My Men Friends

I first learned to appreciate my male friends when I was a boy playing team sports. It became clear that it was our combined efforts which got us down the field, put the ball in the hoop, or brought in a run. I gained great respect for a teammate who made a good block, a great catch, or a move so swift and accurate that the threat of our opponent's scoring was immediately put to rest. It felt great to acknowledge each other's contributions and to be acknowledged, regardless of whether we won or lost the game. After the game we would sit around in the locker room or on the bus ride home, talking about the game and all the great plays, missed opportunities and/or big mistakes. Even in teasing about a goof-up, there was support, reassurance, and encouragement.

It is most often in our play and recreation that we find ourselves able to be more relaxed, vulnerable, and intimate with our men friends. One of my favorite recreational gatherings is my weekly doubles tennis group. These times are high-spirited and lighthearted. We play hard, and we laugh a lot, teasing and joking as a way of expressing our affection. From this tennis group of friends, we plan hiking, boating, dinner parties, and other gatherings where we come together for the good feelings shared. This group is a spinoff of "The Ordway Raiders," a very informal group of hikers, sailors, and storytellers. I have had the pleasure of being with them for many happy outings and parties for almost twenty-five years. I am warmed to be called "Uncle" by my Raider buddies. This nickname was bestowed upon me by Peter, adopted by Greg and later picked up by Ash, John, and Lew, on the trails and on the courts. Each of these men have special strengths and qualities of gentleness which I admire, and I continue to learn from each of them. I am drawn to the vitality of my men friends like iron shavings to a magnet. I like to be in the presence of their energy.

I am particularly blessed to count my four sons among my close friends. They often join me with other men friends for hiking, playing music, or a nickel, dime, and quarter poker game. For the past three or four summers, two or more of them have been team members with me in a summer softball league. Involvement in recreational activities has played, and continues to play, a very large part in contributing to my sense of well-being. I initiate these contacts with my men friends and respond to their invitations for a get-together. These times are often funny and raucous, sometimes quiet and reassuring, and always great fun, as we gather in friendship. When I am among my men friends, I experience a feeling which is best described by the word "camaraderie," which I define as:

The spirit generated among people who gather together in mutual respect and common purpose.

The bonding together of men has roots in early tribes who joined together for hunting, gathering, and defense. These were primal support groups. Survival was favored by such teamwork. As these early men were successful in defense, or in hunting or harvesting, there developed celebrations and rituals to acknowledge their bounty. Friendships formed in appreciation for the support (often lifesaving I imagine) which was provided by a companion. Men danced and chanted together to celebrate and acknowledge this. Camaraderie stems from just such bonding, and is characterized by the high spirits of encouragement, enthusiasm, confidence, and unity. I am sure that women experience this gender-bonding and cohesive spirit of camaraderie in parallel ways, although men probably think they "coined" the term.

Play: An Avenue to Intimacy

Intimacy among men has not been the norm in our culture: our models are few and far between. Emotional closeness may trigger feelings of homophobia. In our culture, boys are conditioned early in adolescence with gay-bashing and from that we learn that if we get too close to another male, we may open ourselves to ridicule and rejection. Touching among men is only really allowed in sports or in a roughhousing, playful way. Otherwise, it is just a good firm handshake, and maybe if you are really a risk taker, a pat on the shoulder. Unfortunately, in much of our adult life, it is not usual for men to acknowledge and support each other. The competitive edge often becomes the competitive wedge.

It is in our play that we add dimensionality and become more whole, more rounded. Play can be a prelude to intimacy. One of the important by-products of play is the opportunity for humor, for being affectionate in teasing, and for reminiscing. Such playfulness is very good for the soul. It is best if it serves as a vehicle for softening the edges for a deeper and fuller sharing of feelings. The danger, of course, is that we might hide out totally or too long in our play and never truly connect person-to-person by sharing those soulful dimensions of ourselves which we too easily keep hidden. But when there is trust and a feeling of safety, it is extremely nurturing to experience the warm feelings of friendship which ensue. It is healing to be with friends with whom I can be myself and with whom I can laugh about all the male behaviors we exhibit around our gains and losses in the "success game." In these light moments, our achievement orientation takes on much less importance. Lightness creates perspective and adds balance. We have known this for a long time, and the wisdom is summed up in the familiar proverb: "All work and no play makes Jack a dull boy."

Stress & Support

Grieving my relationship loss was easier when I shared my true feelings with friends who listened—friends who asked "How are you doing?" and who really cared about my answer, even if I told them that "Things are not going great." Friendship means you will be there for each other in good times and in bad. This kind of support is extremely important. To feel that love, acceptance, and sense of belonging among our peers and family is to be blessed. From these friends and family, I have gained strength, courage, humor, and a sense of belonging as I have moved along my path from boyhood to manhood. When times are particularly stressful for me, being with my men friends makes my burden a little lighter.

Models & Mentors

Most of the significant activities and undertakings which I have pursued in my life have been stimulated by my admiring someone who has set a good example. My first important model (and thus a mentor) was my brother Loren, and I dedicate this chapter to him because so much of the rest of my life has been built on those early learnings. I admired the way he coped with life, and in many ways I copied him in my formative years. As a boy, I learned how to be in my peer group from Loren, and his example set the tone for friendships which have followed.

For most of us, men and women alike, there will often be

one person who stands out as our most important teacher, model, and guide. For men, it might be a dad, a brother, an uncle, a coach, a teacher, or some other man you admire for the way they cope with life. Hopefully it is a man we can get close to, someone you can know and be known by.

I was lucky. In college, I met Dr. William R. ("Cherry") Parker. He became my chief mentor. Cherry the professor, the clinician, the friend, was the same enthusiastic, loving, and warm man in whatever hat he was wearing. I was drawn to his joy and his humor, his exuberance and love of life, and his deeply spiritual messages of love. His laughter was contagious and his purposeful mission in life as a psychologist and speech pathologist seemed to me to represent a way of being that I could believe in and envision for myself. I felt his love and respect in a way that I had not known before. I was validated as a person, even prized, and this was the greatest gift of all. Cherry believed in me, and because of him, I came to believe more in myself and my possibilities.

It wasn't just me. I was part of a group of mostly male students who were drawn to study with him. I can name more than thirty others who were inspired by Cherry to develop their professional careers through doctoral study. Our paths were illuminated by the very force of his encouragement, his teachings, and his example. His message of love continues to be an inspiration to me.

Empowerment: To Be Believed in As a Person

This matter of Cherry Parker believing in me and helping me to see that which is good in life, has affected me profoundly. My relationships are greatly enhanced because I respond to the strengths and qualities in others. In my work with clients and with graduate students, I know that one of the greatest gifts I give them is to have them come to know that I believe in them. The more I believe in their capacity to grow and transcend their current dilemmas, the more they believe in themselves and do grow and transcend. This is the gift of encouragement, and it is extremely empowering. Because I had, and still have, models and mentors who continue to encourage me, I find myself wanting to pass this gift on to others. I have a strong belief that there is goodness and creative expression in people which is waiting to be developed.

There are those who hold more cynical views. They would remind me that there is ample evidence of evil and incompetence in the world. I know very well that there are individuals who have themselves been badly abused and those who never received the love and respect so essential for developing their sense of worth. As a psychologist, I remain hopeful that those who have not had support and encouragement in their past, will find healthy ways to create the love they need to grow toward their full potential.

No Age or Gender Limit

I seek models of health, vitality, and competence. For me, age and gender do not present boundaries or limits to my openness to people from whom I can learn. I am often amazed at how much I learn from my four sons. Each of them has qualities which I admire, and seeing these qualities makes them come more alive in me. I continue to be touched by any person whose competence, courage, or sensitivity I admire.

Yesterday I spent some time with my friend and neighbor Norm, who in his seventies, is twenty years my senior and continues to be a model for me. Norm faces aging with courage and grace, and I learn much from his positive outlook on life even as he has faced major physical setbacks in the last few years. Last week I had lunch with my friend and colleague Jack, who being ten years my senior, is thinking about retiring. He talked about his feelings and his dreams about possibilities as he faces this transition. I asked what he was doing to stay in shape. He said that he swims and wants to get back into indoor swimming now that summer is closing. I suggested joining him for regular workouts and he welcomed the idea. So now I have another opportunity to know Jack, and to be known by him. My friend Dugald sets another good example for me. Nearly eighty, his goal this summer has been to complete hiking to the peaks of all the four-thousand-foot mountains in New Hampshire. Skiing with him this winter he reminded me that he takes things a little slower, and I say to myself: "This is what I want to be like when I am his age."

We all need contact with elders in our lives. There is a special kind of learning we take from their experienced perspective. I honor their ability to survive. There are times that it takes great courage and endurance to face life. Elders have known loss and disappointment, and if they are fortunate they might also know great joy and celebrations in life. This knowledge which they possess is there for our asking. We must only be open to their wisdom to receive this special grace. Our elders have a gift for us which no others have to give.

From elders, something is transferred to us which speaks of our evolution throughout generations. My father Wayne, and my father's father (Henry Clay Webb) and his father (George Washington Webb) most assuredly passed down their personal ways of being, as I now do for my sons and they for their progeny, and so on down the line. For me this holds a rich spiritual meaning as a sense of connectedness to and being in one's life stream through time. I suspect my tone of voice, gesture, facial expression or posture may all reveal traces of my ancestors. These things are learned in ways which are beyond speaking; ways which are modeled by action not instruction.

I don't fully understand how it is that being wounded takes us deeper into ourselves, but from my experience and observations I make the following assumptions.

- When we are wounded by a personal crisis upsetting our sense of self and how we see ourselves in the world, we seek the solace of our own gender.

- As we open ourselves to others, we are able to let go of our pain.
- There is a healing energy created and transmitted among friends which promotes our recovery to wholeness. This energy is expressed as caring, acceptance, patience, faith, understanding, and much more. It is this love energy of the human spirit which is both tangible and ethereal that allows us to be real, and to be healed from the pain of grieving.
- By risking being known, we relax our egos and lay down our armor.
- We are re-refined, re-created, re-paired, and re-stored by the love and caring within our friendships.

XIV. Taking Action ✍

...there is a very human urge to explore our boundaries
and to actualize our potential.
It is as true in the geography of our mind
as it is in the physical universe.

This is the final stage of your recovery. It is time to act on your plan, on your ideas, your dreams, and your images which are emerging. These are new stages, new textures, and fresh experiences. Your plan is not a fixed blueprint, but an openness to discovery. It is what I call a "Magellan Consciousness," a willingness to explore frontiers.

Be an explorer! Give yourself the gift of yourself by stretching your ideas, flexing your attitudes, and discovering the edges of your growth. This is our natural quest to improve the quality of our lives. Set your sails for your new world in this final stage of recovery as your old harbors and anchorages from your previous relationship fade over the horizon.

This is a time for you to be pro-active instead of re-active. It is a time to rise up with energy and renewed faith in yourself and your own growth process. It is a time to listen to what is going on inside yourself that wants to create newness.

Singled Out

Being single was a new experience for me. Most of the major connections to my couple-friends world and social life had all been with Winter. It wasn't that I felt ostracized, I just found myself not invited when former friends had gatherings which brought together couples.[29] If I wanted to belong to that circle again, I would need to have a partner. This void was a painful motivator to get me into taking action toward creating a new life for myself. It became an exciting time of exploration and discovery. The more I dated and met new people, the more my social life expanded and the more my loss receded into history.

Considering Wholeness and Wellness

We are whole integrated selves and in taking our most effective action, we must embrace our wholeness in a balanced way. We must take care of our bodies:
- with sleep, rest, and good nutrition.
- with healthy sexual and sensual experiences.
- with physical exercise.
- with wilderness encounters.

We must take care of our minds:
- with watchful observations of our best options.
- with disciplined efforts to choose.
- with patience, understanding, and self-acceptance.
- with responsible behavior.

and

We must take care of our spirits:
- with quiet time to seek our meaning and purpose.
- with connecting to our fellow humans on the planet in a mutually enriching way.
- with graceful responses to the music and artistic experiences of our humanity.

and by
- standing in ecstatic wonder of the universe.

We must take care of our social lives:
- with intimate times with family and friends.
- with meeting our needs to belong to a community.
- with participation in purposeful service to others.

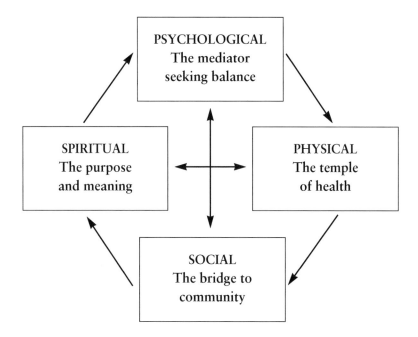

"First be a good animal."

A beginning place for me is encouraged by the above quote by George E. Sheehan.[30] It is important for me to continue to develop and express my physical being. If I am playing tennis, sailing, skiing, hiking, or working in the woods, I have a certain loss of consciousness about my psychological pain. My immersion into physical activities provides fun and intimate times with friends and family, keeps my body in reasonable tone, and gives me a sense of well-being. Physical well-being is the foundation for our wholeness.

I need to schedule physical activities and not to leave them to chance happenings. At my age and stage, I try to do daily stretching and breathing exercises as a follow-up to my morning shower and to go for walks several times a week. All these activities provide a defense against depression. Most of my physical activity involves me in social contact, and so I get a double benefit. Making friends and maintaining friendships is an active process which I initiate to nourish this important dimension of my life. I often invite a friend to lunch or to dinner, and out of these interactions comes the ideas for a tennis game or a hiking, sailing, or skiing trip. As a single person, this initiating also brings the possibilities for dating and intimacy. The key for me is in taking the initiative. Somewhere in my life I have learned that if I want something to happen, I need to take responsibility for trying to make that something happen.

All–Fronts Assault

It is not an exaggeration to say that there are a thousand things to do: Let your stream of consciousness rain down as you image yourself doing:

aerobics, art classes
bicycling, baking
canoeing, church
driving, digging, and daydreaming
enjoying everything
fun things with a friend
and so on through the alphabet....

Think of all the verbs for being and doing, all the things that humans can do. We can try anything; there is no end to what we can do.

I'm always touched when I see or hear about some person, who may appear to be severely handicapped, doing something which takes great courage or perseverance. I'm thinking of how I felt when I saw a person whose arms and legs were paralyzed, painting a picture with a brush held in his teeth. I have a special admiration and respect for persons who have lost one of their legs and yet who learn to ski very well.

A few weeks ago, I listened to the results of the Boston marathon. The winner of the wheelchair division was a former pole-vaulting champion whose legs were paralyzed after a tragic accident. He said something like the following over the air:

> *Before my accident, I could do a thousand things.*
> *Now I can only do about 900. I focus on the 900*
> *that I still can do.*

This takes courage, and it takes grace and commitment. Perhaps the word that captures this is *Grit*.

An all-fronts approach is to commit to your health, your vitality, your imagination, and creativity in all that you choose to give yourself to. The truly awake state is to act, to create, to experience. Do something!

- Call a friend.
- Take up golf or gardening or the like.
- Learn to play a musical instrument.
- Water the lawn.
- Notice the roses and trees.
- Smell the smells.
- Take some deep breaths.
- Go to meetings
  workshops
  church
  parties and dances.
- Go out of your way to meet people.

William Glasser[31] said that it is hard to be depressed if you are doing something. He said we have to walk the walk, and not just talk the talk. Just to get up out of your chair and to do something is an improvement over sitting and feeling sorry for yourself. I also like what John F. Kennedy said once in quoting some ancient wisdom: "The journey of a thousand miles starts with the first step." Take it!

Building for Success

A good thing to remember in choosing to take action is to bite off a piece you can chew. What you want is to have success, and this might start with small choices at first.

When you succeed in doing what you set out to do, you create a new image of yourself and of your world. For example:

> *If I climb a ladder, I have a larger view of my world from the top. If I visualize this at a later time, I can see myself on top of the ladder, and this memory stimulates a positive reinforcement for my achievement. I can feel good about myself for each step I take.*

Will Power & Want Power: Your Choice

There is such a thing as will power. In your life, you may or may not have experienced much of it, but it is available for you to use. Here is the key for getting in touch with your will power. First, make certain that what you want is desirable.

Believe what you want is possible.

Believe that you have the capability to achieve what you want.

Believe that you deserve it just because you are human and you are alive.

Make a plan to achieve it...

with specific goals,

with specific dates.

This will help you see your path on this.

Make a commitment to the plan.

Start with the first step.

If you fall, take a smaller step which you can achieve.

Recognize your achievement with self-praise:

tell yourself something good,

make an affirmation.

Continue on your path.

Push yourself a little to reach your goals.

If you don't know where to start in taking your action, do the following exercises:

- List three specific behaviors which have worked well for you under difficult circumstances in the past.

_____

_____

_____

- Write down three things you need for yourself.

_____

_____

_____

- And, three things you want for yourself.

_____

_____

_____

If your lists are not as positive as you would like, treat yourself to a rewrite, and dare to dream how you would really like your life to be. Daydream about letting yourself receive the things you need and want and then cooperate with that daydream image by taking responsibility for making these things happen in your life to get you where you want to be. When you are clear about your needs and wants, and what works for you, you can begin to identify your first steps.

Write these first steps down as a way of putting teeth in your contract with yourself. Share these commitments with a friend, or your counselor. Going public reinforces your commitment because we are conditioned not to let down people who believe in us. We need to save face. If your commitments to yourself are a secret, it is too easy to ignore them without much consequence except that then we can see that we were not really very committed, and quietly be disappointed in ourselves.

A THREE-STEP PLAN OF ACTION
I AM WILLING TO COMMIT TO
IN ORDER TO GET ON WITH MY LIFE.

Step One: _____

_____

_____

Date I will start: _____

Step Two: _____

_____

_____

Date I will start: _____

Step Three: _____

_____

_____

Date I will start: _____

Signed: _____

Date: _____

Witness: _____

Date: _____

XV. Fifty Ways to Love Your Leaver ✍

Admit the hurt, Curt,
Face the pain, Jane,
Try not to deny, Di
Make a new plan, Ann,
Everything's all right, Dwight
Just let go, Joe
Find your own key, Lee
and set yourself free.[32]

I was getting on a plane to go teach summer school in Colorado and I was feeling good about myself as a bachelor. Even though I had not found my new mate, I was enjoying the search. Winter and I had now been separated for three or four years, and I was aware that I could love her as a person and that I was no longer interested in her as being my mate. I could love her without being in love with her. Having let go of Winter with love, I was thinking how she had left me, or had been the leaver, and Paul Simon's song came into my head in this twisted kind of way. It immediately occurred to me that this idea would be a good theme for a book on relationship loss. The Simon song is also about relationship loss, but with tongue-in-cheek humor, he poked fun at our own male consciousness of the time, by providing a list of rather non-feeling and non-grieving approaches. You will recall: "Just hop on the bus, Gus / Drop off the key, Lee," and other somewhat calloused suggestions for males leaving relationships and being "cool." The song seemed to advocate an essentially non-caring and non-communicative way of initiating a breakup.

As I took my seat on the airplane, I began to write down as many loving ways as I could think of about relationships breaking up. It was the beginning of this book, and as the chapters unfolded, I expanded on the initial ideas and developed the following fifty ways:

THE HEALING PATH	THE STUCK PATH
Do:	**Do Not:**
Let in the truth and deal with as much reality as you are able to and still cope.	Get stuck in denial.
Acknowledge the caring and depth you once shared, and the loss you feel.	Discount your caring in order to save face. You only devalue your own experience.
Find support with friends and family when you can, and a professional counselor when necessary.	Act so tough and invulnerable that you go it alone. This will not impress anyone that matters to you in the long run.
Release the pain of your hurt with these support persons.	Hold it in, it will only come out later as anger and blame.
Be congruent (honest with yourself and others).	Put on the mask of "I don't care." It doesn't fit with the depth of love you had, and it's phony.
Know you have choices and can make them	Lock yourself into patterned or programmed behavior such as playing the "victim" or the "vindictive."
Choose behaviors that are productive. Know that attitudes and feelings will follow behavior.	Strike out in angry retribution. This contributes to your confusion and tension, and will tend to make you more depressed.

THE HEALING PATH	THE STUCK PATH
Do:	**Do Not:**
Try to understand your former mate's feelings and experiences.	Seek self-righteousness. It will only alienate you from others.
Accept responsibility for your life.	Blame others or circumstances for what happens to you.
Let go of anger by looking at all your feelings.	Hold on to anger. It will spill out in all your relationships. Carrying anger is a burden.
Accept that this person you once shared love with is no longer in that same place. He or she has changed. That is the reality!	Withdraw and retreat into bitterness and judgment. These toxic feelings will only continue to recycle your stuckness.
Let go and wish your former partner well.	Try to hold on to this person. In the first place, it is not possible and secondly, it only serves to keep you stuck.
Trust and risk being vulnerable to love again.	Give up on trust, you will be giving up on intimacy.
Get on with building your new world of relationships.	Withdraw or sit around and mope. Isolation breeds depression.
Accept yourself as a changing, growing, fallible human being.	Live your life, with inflexible rigid rights, wrongs, always, and nevers.

THE HEALING PATH	THE STUCK PATH
Do:	**Do Not:**

Do something nice for your-self each day. Celebrate new beginnings as opportunities.	Seek self-pity. Don't assume the world is against you. If you are against yourself, the world will join you.
See yourself as the program-mer of your mind. You are in charge and how things turn out for you depends on how you set them up.	Let others dominate your choices and program your life with should's and ought to's for the sake of others.
Take on the challenge of optimism. It will work magic for you if you are open to it. Confidence builds confidence.	Let yourself fall into pessimism and self-doubting. Bitter negative energy that persists will only poison you.
Take away learnings from your own experience.	Fail to learn from your experience.
Cooperate with your inner wisdom as you seek to balance your body, mind, social, and spirit integration.	Just listen to your head or just to your body. Isolating parts of yourself is putting blinders on the wholeness of your experience.
Acknowledge your own strengths and give yourself the credit you deserve.	Discount or put yourself down, it will be a barrier to your growth.
Become an observer of your own behavior and look for the big picture and patterns to get balance.	Stick your head in the sand and refuse to see what you are doing or going to do about what you are doing.

THE HEALING PATH Do:	THE STUCK PATH Do Not:
Learn to assert yourself effectively, recognizing your feelings, needs, desires, and reactions.	Be aggressive or take on a passive or passive/aggressive pattern. In the long run, these will all be counter-productive.
Be willing to make commitments to yourself and to significant others.	Settle for less than what is out there for what you want in your life.
Love yourself.	Even consider the alternatives.

You can see by now that this book is really about fifty thousand ways to love yourself. If you love yourself, it will follow that you will love your leaver.

Beyond Forgiveness...Full Circle to Gladness

This is the frosting on the cake. It is when you realize that you are glad not to be with your former mate. You have changed, and she or he has changed, and you have decided that you have big differences and incompatible priorities. Acknowledge all the beauty and love you shared and know that nothing need ever diminish that. You will come to know that your leaver did you a big favor by leaving since she or he no longer shares a common dream with you. Think how awful it would be to continue in a relationship full of struggle and indifference. It was just a wonderful part of your past.

Love is the best way to be your full self.
Be Joyous in giving your love
 and
It will be returned in fullness.
Celebrate your recovery and rebirth.

Epilogue:
An Update on My Life ☙

Winter and I are still friends. I don't see her much anymore, but occasionally over the years we have found time to have lunch together or sit down for a good visit over a glass of wine. These are always warm and friendly encounters, and we both come away acknowledging our appreciation for what we shared. I have continued to be genuinely interested in her life, and her family.

Completing this book closes the grieving and recovery process for me. This transition has particular sweetness for me since I have just married Leslie, the woman I have loved for the past six years. It is more than coincidental that I started dating Leslie about the time I started writing this book. It is interesting timing that our marriage has occurred just as I finish this book—two powerful marker events, one of completion, one a beginning.

For me, one of the most important dimensions of Leslie's and my wedding was that my four sons served as my best men. Their participation and support was a final ceremonial acknowledgement of the closing of my bachelorhood and the opening of my new married life with Leslie.

The night before the wedding, my sons and I got together with a few friends for a bachelor party at Ben and Sara's house on the Lamprey River. We gathered around an open fire, and my good buddy Bert orchestrated a sharing of feelings which was very powerful. Ben had brought along a talking stick from Native American tradition, and as the stick was passed among my friends, my sons, and myself, we took our speaking opportunity as a time to reflect on our feelings. My sons spoke from their hearts of their feelings of good wishes, and also of their pain that our original family had not survived, and was, in fact, now going through a major transition. It was this expression of pain that made this sharing so powerful and so important for me. To avoid the expression of, or to gloss over, their pain would have somehow buried something in a lie.

Their mother, my former wife, and I have remained on friendly terms, and have shared the joys and concerns of parenting. As a family over these years, we have often gathered together for special holidays, our sons' birthdays, graduations, and so on. In some ways, this amiable relationship held up a fantasy of hope for my sons that their mother and I might get back together. While there has been no serious consideration of that happening, it is understandable that they should wish for it at some level. Divorce has to be an extremely painful loss for children who love both parents.

Even as my sons held the talking stick by the fire and shared their feelings of loss in this transition time, there was also the expression of great support and love in their sincere good wishes which I felt from each. When I shared this with Leslie, she astutely observed, "Working through the pain strengthens all relationships."

At our wedding the next day, the rings were passed from Chris to John to Michael and to David and on to me and Leslie. This hands-on, tangible–touching was for me a powerful symbol of their blessing and their support for our marriage.

I continue to face new challenges, questions, and uncertainties. I face them with hope and with a peaceful feeling, knowing that I can continue to sculpt my own experience.

My challenge is to be all I can be...

> *in this marriage;*
> *as a possible new father of children with Leslie;*
> *as a parent of my four sons,*
> *and grandparent to their children;*
> *as a brother and a friend;*
> *as a professor, a counselor, and a writer.*

I invite you to join me with your challenges...

> *to claim your own strength and to take*
> *the courage to discover your own best way*
> *of expressing your love.*

My wish for all who will hear this message:

> *Be of good strength and good cheer along your*
> *journey to the full and happy life you deserve.*

Notes ℘

Introduction

1. Victor Frankl, *Man's Search for Meaning* (New York: Washington Square Press, 1963).
2. Barbara Peeks, "Children and Teens," *The Advocate*, a newsletter of the Children and Teens Special Interest Network, 1990. For more information, contact Barbara Peeks at the Family and Childrens Center, 221 South Jeffers, Suite 4, North Platte, Nebraska, 69101, U.S.A.

Chapter I

3. Elizabeth Kubler-Ross, *On Death and Dying* (New York: McMillan, 1969).

Chapter II

4. For starters, readers are recommended to read Sam Keen's *Fire in the Belly: On Being a Man* (New York: Bantam, 1991), and Robert Bly's *Iron John*, (Boston, Addison Wesley, 1990).
5. From the song entitled, *Already Gone*, by Jack Tempchin and Robb Strandlund.

Chapter III

6. From the song entitled, *The Rose*, by Amanda McBroom.

Chapter IV

7. J. Krishnamurti, *Education and the Significance of Life* (New York: Harper Row, 1953).
8. I am indebted to William R. "Cherry" Parker for illuminating this idea so powerfully in his teachings. His thoughts are written in his classic book entitled, *Prayer Can Change Your Life* (New York: Prentice-Hall 1957).
9. For a more complete treatment of this idea, see Herb Goldberg's, *The Inner Male: Overcoming Roadblocks to Intimacy*

(New York: New American Library, 1989).

10. Norman Cousins, *Anatomy of an Illness* (New York: Norton, 1979).

11. Carl Rogers, *On Personal Power* (New York, Delta, 1977). I also recommend his book, *On Becoming Partners* (New York: Dell, 1977) for a wide perspective on marriage and its alternatives.

Chapter V

12. Joan Borysenko, *Fire in the Soul* (New York: Warner Books, 1993). Chapter Seven on Forgiveness and Freedom speaks of how anger is crippling if we need to make ourselves right at the expense of making others wrong.

13. Gay Hendricks is an educator and author who has made significant contributions in the area of transpersonal psychology. See *The Centering Book* and *The Centered Teacher* among others. Most recently he and his wife Kathlyn completed *Conscious Loving: A Couples Guide to Co-Commitment* (Bantam Press, 1993).

14. Herb Goldberg, *The Inner Male: Overcoming Roadblocks to Intimacy* (New York: New American Library, 1987).

15. Thomas More, *Care of the Soul* (New York: Harper Collins, 1992).

16. Sam Keen, *Fire in the Belly: On Being a Man* (New York, Bantam, 1991). Chapter Ten deals with the journey of numbness to manly grief.

Chapter VI

17. Carl Rogers, *On Becoming a Person* (Boston, Houghton Mifflin, 1961).

18. Tom Gordon, *Parent Effectiveness Training* (New York: Wyden Press, 1972).

Chapter VII

19. B. F. Skinner, *Walden Two* (New York: MacMillan, 1976).

Chapter IX

20. Ideas for this scale were generated by others who have done

research in the area of stress. One example would be the *Family Inventory of Life Events and Changes* by Hamilton I. McCubbin and Joan M. Peterson from the University of Minnesota, St. Paul, Minnesota, 55108.

21. Sam Keen, *Apology for Wonder* (New York: Harper & Row, 1969).
22. Robin Casargian, *Forgiveness: A Bold Choice for a Peaceful Heart* (New York: Bantam, 1992).
23. Martin Seligman, *Learned Optimism: How to Change Your Mind and Life* (New York: Pocket Books, 1990). The idea of choice is very well explained in Chapter One entitled, "Two Ways of Looking at Life."

Chapter X
24. Abraham Maslow, *The Psychology of Being* (Princeton: D. Van Nostrand, 1962).
25. Martin Seligman, *Learned Optimism: How to Change Your Mind and Life* (New York: Pocket Books, 1990).

Chapter XI
26. Victor Frankl, *Man's Search for Meaning* (New York: Washington Square Press, 1963).
27. David Burns, *The Feeling Good Handbook* (New York: Morrow, 1989).
28. Robert Rosenthal and Lenore Jacobson, *Pygmalion in the Classroom* (Manchester, NH: Irvington Publisher, 1992).

Chapter XIV
29. For an account on singleness, see Bruce Fisher's *Rebuilding When Your Relationship Ends* (San Luis Obispo: Impact, 1981).
30. From a lecture by George Sheehan, author of *Running and Being* (New York: Simon & Shuster, 1978).
31. William Glasser is the author of *Reality Therapy* (New York, NY: Harper & Row, 1965) and several other important books which stress personal responsibility. He is the director for Institute for Reality Therapy in Canoga Park, CA.
32. With credit to Paul Simon for his song, *Fifty Ways to Leave Your Lover.*

Bibliography ✍

A. Alvarez, Life After Marriage: *Love in an Age of Divorce* (New York, NY: Simon and Schuster, 1981).

S. P. Andrews, *Love, Marriage and Divorce, and the Sovereignty of the Individual* (New York, NY: Source Book Press, 1972).

R. Austin, *How to Make it with Another Person* (New York, NY: MacMillan, 1976).

O. Ayalon, *Chain Reaction: Children and Divorce* (London; Bristol, PA: J. Kingsley Publishers, 1993).

G. Bach & P. Wyden, *The Intimate Enemy: How to Fight Fair in Love & Marriage* (New York, NY: Avon, 1968).

J. Belovitch, Editor, *Making Remarriage Work* (Lexington, MA: Lexington Books, 1987).

C. Berman, *Preparing to Remarry* (New York, NY: Public Affairs Committee, 1987).

J. & S. Bloom-Feshbach, *The Psychology of Separation and Loss: Perspectives on Development, Life Transitions, and Clinical Practice* (San Francisco, CA: Jossey-Bass, 1987).

P. Bohannan, *Divorce and After* (Garden City, NY: Doubleday, 1970).

J. Borysenko, *Guilt is the Teacher, Love is the Lesson* (New York, NY: Warner Books, 1990).

L. M. Brammer, *How to Cope with Life Transition: The Challenge of Personal Change* (New York, NY: Hemisphere Publishing Corp., 1991).

S. M. Campbell, *The Couple's Journey: Intimacy as a Path to Wholeness* (San Luis Obispo, CA: Impact Publishers, 1980).

R. Casarjian, *Forgiveness: A Bold Choice for a Peaceful Heart* (New York, NY: Bantam, 1992).

A. J. Cherlin, *Marriage, Divorce, Remarriage* (Cambridge, MA: Harvard University Press, 1981).

D. Cole, *After Great Pain: A New Life Emerges* (New York, NY: Summit Books, 1992).

Colgrove, Bloomfield & McWilliams, *How to Survive the Loss of a Love* (New York, NY: Leo Press, 1976).

J. F. Crosby, *Illusion and Disillusion: The Self in Love and Marriage* (Belmont, CA: Wadsworth Publishing Company, 1991).

J. G. Cull, *Deciding on Divorce: Personal and Family Considerations* (Springfield, IL: Thomas, 1974).

M. Edwards, *The Challenge of Being Single* (New York, NY: Hawthorn, 1974).

B. Fisher, *Rebuilding When Your Relationship Ends* (San Luis Obispo, CA: Impact Publishers, 1981).

H. E. Fisher, *Anatomy of Love: The Natural History of Monogamy, Adultery and Divorce* (New York, NY: Norton, 1992).

J. Fuller, *Space: The Scrapbook of My Divorce* (Connecticut: Fawcett, 1973).

R. Gardner, *The Parents Book about Divorce* (Garden City, NJ: Doubleday and Company, 1977).

C. Giampolo, *Letting Go* (New York, NY: Bantam, 1990).

W. J. Goode, *After Divorce* (Westport, CT: Greenwood Press, 1978).

B. S. Gordon, *The First Year Alone* (Dublin, NH: W.L. Bauhan, 1986).

J. M. Gottman, *What Predicts Divorce? The Relationship Between Marital Processes and Marital Outcomes* (Hillsdale, NJ: Lawrence Erlbaum Associates, 1994).

J. Gray, *Men are from Mars, Women are from Venus: A Practical Guide for Improving Communication and Getting What You Want in Your Relationships* (New York, NY: HarperCollins, 1992).

E. Grollman, *Explaining Divorce to Children* (Boston, MA: Beacon Press, 1969).

G. Hendricks & K. Hendricks, *Conscious Loving: The Journey to Co-Commitment* (New York, NY: Bantam, 1990).

H. Hendrix, *Getting the Love You Want: A Guide for Couples* (New York, NY: Harper-Row, 1988).

Barbara Hirsch, *Divorce: What a Woman Needs to Know* (Chicago, IL: Henry Reginery Co., 1973).

M. Hunt, and Hunt, *The Divorce Experience: A New Look at the Formerly Married* (New York, NY: McGraw-Hill, 1977).

G. F. Jacobson, *The Multiple Crises of Marital Separation and Divorce* (New York, NY: Grune & Stratton, 1983).

G. Jampolsky, *Teach Only Love: The Seven Principles of Attitudinal Healing* (New York, NY: Bantam, 1983).

Claudia Jewett, *Helping Children Cope with Separation & Loss* (Harvard, MA: The Harvard Common Press, 1982).

S. J. Katz, & A. Liu, *False Love: And Other Romantic Illusions* (New York, NY: Ticknor & Fields, 1988).

Sam Keen, *Fire in the Belly: On Being a Man* (New York, NY: Bantam, 1991).

S. Kessler, *The American Way of Divorce: Prescriptions for Change* (Chicago, IL: Nelson-Hall, 1975).

M. Krantzler, *Creative Divorce: A New Opportunity for Personal Growth* (New York, NY: M. Evans, 1973).

Elizabeth Kubler-Ross, *On Death and Dying* (New York, NY: Macmillan, 1969).

C. Leavenworth, *Love and Commitment: You Don't Have to Settle for Less* (Englewood Cliffs, NJ: Prentice Hall, 1981).

J. Lee, *I Don't Want to be Alone* (Deerfield Beach, FL: Health Communications, Inc., 1990).

N. Leick, *Healing Pain: Attachment, Loss, and Grief Therapy* (London; New York: Routledge, 1991).

J. Littlewood, *Aspects of Grief: Bereavement in Adult Life* (London; New York: Tavistock/Routledge, 1992).

R. K. Moffett, *Dealing with Divorce* (Boston, MA: Little, Brown, 1976).

N. O'Connor, *Letting Go with Love: The Grieving Process* (Tucson, AZ: La Mariposa Press, 1984).

E. Ogg, *Divorce: Legal and Personal Concerns* (New York, NY: Public Affairs Committee, 1987).

E. Price, *Getting Through the Night: Finding Your Way After the Loss of a Loved One* (New York, NY: Dial Press, 1982).

S. J. Price, *Divorce* (Newbury Park, CA: Sage Publications, 1988).

C. Robertson, *Divorce and Decision Making, A Woman's Guide* (Chicago, IL: Follett, 1980).

Carl R. Rogers, *Becoming Partners: Marriage and its Alternatives* (New York, NY: Delacorte Press, 1972).

Carl R. Rogers, *On Personal Power* (New York, NY: Delta, 1977).

R. Sager, *Marriage Contracts and Couples Therapy: Hidden Forces in Intimate Relationships* (New York, NY: Brunner/Mazel Publishers, 1980).

L. Salk, *What Every Child Would Like Parents to Know About Divorce* (New York, NY: Harper & Row, 1978).

M. Scarf, *Intimate Partners: Patterns in Love and Marriage* (New York, NY: Random House, 1987).

Martin Seligman, *Learned Optimism: How to Change Your Mind and Your Life* (New York, NY: Pocket Books, 1990).

S. S. Simring, *Marriage and Divorce, a Contemporary Perspective* (New York, NY: Guilford Press, 1984).

J. Sinberg, *Divorce is a Grown Up Problem: A Book About Divorce for Young Children and Their Parents* (New York, NY: Avon, 1978).

L. Singer, *Beyond Loss: A Practical Guide Through Grief to a Meaningful Life* (New York, NY: Dutton, 1988).

C. R. Snyder, *Coping with Negative Life Events: Clinical and Social Psychological Perspectives* (New York, NY: Plenum Press, 1987).

R. Stuart, *Helping Couples Change: A Social Learning Approach to Marital Therapy* (New York, NY: Guilford Press, 1980).

D. Vaughan, *Uncoupling: Turning Points in Intimate Relationships* (New York, NY: Oxford University Press, 1986).

S. S. Volgy, editor, *Women and Divorce/Men and Divorce: Gender Differences in Separation, Divorce, and Remarriage* (New York, NY: Haworth Press, 1991).

J. S. Wallerstein, *Surviving the Breakup: How Children and Parents Cope with Divorce* (New York, NY: Basic Books, 1980).

R. Weiss, *Marital Separation* (New York, NY: Basic Books, 1975).

J. Welwood, *Journey of the Hearts: Intimate Relationships and the Path of Love* (New York, NY: HarperCollins, 1990).

Janet Woijitz, *Struggle for Intimacy* (Pompano Beach, FL: Health Communications, 1985).

Women in Transition, Inc., *Women in Transition: A Feminist Handbook on Separation and Divorce* (New York, NY: Scribner, 1975).